Medical Miracles of the Qur'ān

Dr. Sharif Kaf Al-Ghazal

THE ISLAMIC FOUNDATION

Published by

The Islamic Foundation
Markfield Conference Centre
Ratby Lane, Markfield
Leicestershire, LE67 9SY, United Kingdom
Tel: 01530 244944/5, Fax: 01530 244946
E-mail: info@islamic-foundation.org.uk
publications@islamic-foundation.com
Website: www.islamic-foundation.org.uk

Quran House, P.O. Box 30611, Nairobi, Kenya

P.M.B. 3193, Kano, Nigeria

British Library Cataloguing-in-Publication Data

Al-Ghazal, Sharif Kaf
    Medical miracles of the Qur'an
    1. Medicine in the Koran
    I. Title   II. Islamic Foundation (Great Britain)
    297.1'22861

ISBN 0 86037 525 0

Cover/Book design & typeset: Nasir Cadir

Dedication

Dedicated to everyone seeking the truth.

Transliteration Table

Arabic Consonants:

Initial, unexpressed medial and final:

ء	ʾ	د	d	ض	ḍ	ك	k
ب	b	ذ	dh	ط	ṭ	ل	l
ت	t	ر	r	ظ	ẓ	م	m
ث	th	ز	z	ع	ʿ	ن	n
ج	j	س	s	غ	gh	هـ	h
ح	ḥ	ش	sh	ف	f	و	w
خ	kh	ص	ṣ	ق	q	ي	y

Vowels, diphthongs, etc.

Short: ＿ a   ＿ i   ＿ u

Long: ‍ـَا ā   ‍ـُو ū   ‍ـِي ī

Diphthongs: ‍ـَوْ aw

‍ـَىْ ay

Contents

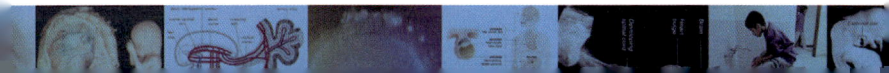

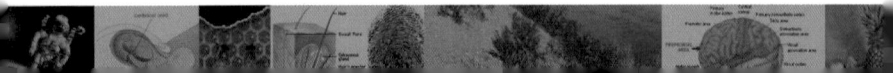

Acknowledgement

I would like to acknowledge the great help Mr. M Madi provided with the English translation and editing of this manuscript.

Introduction

Fourteen centuries ago, Allah (SWT) sent down the Qur'ān to mankind as a book of guidance. He called upon people to be guided to the truth by adhering to this book. From the day of its revelation to the Day of Judgement, this last divine book, the Holy Qur'ān, will remain the sole guide, faith and a methodology of life for humanity.

Allah says in the Qur'ān:

> *Surely this Qur'ān guides to the way that is straightest and gives good tidings to the believers who do deeds of righteousness, that theirs shall be a great wage.* (17:9)

The matchless style of the Qur'ān and its superior wisdom are definite evidence that it is the word of God. In addition, the Qur'ān possesses many miraculous attributes proving that it is a revelation from God. One of these attributes is the fact that a number of scientific truths that we have only been able to uncover with the aid of twentieth century technology, were stated in the Qur'ān 1,400 years ago. Of course the Qur'ān is not a

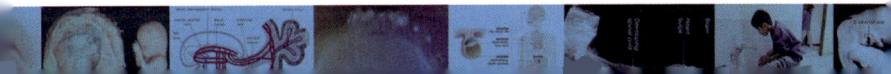

book of science. However, many scientific facts that are expressed in an extremely concise and profound manner in its verses have only been discovered in recent years. These facts could not have been known at the time of the Qur'ān's revelation, and this furnishes still more proof that the Qur'ān is the word of God.

In order to understand the scientific miracle of the Qur'ān, we must first take a look at the level of science pertaining at the time this holy book was revealed. This was in the seventh century, when many superstitious and groundless beliefs, at least where scientific issues were concerned, pervaded Arab society. Lacking the technology to examine the universe and nature, these early Arabs believed in legends inherited from past generations. They supposed, for example, that mountains supported the sky above. They believed that the earth was flat and that there were high mountains at both its ends. It was thought that these mountains were pillars that kept the vault of heaven high above.

With the arrival of the Qur'ān, however, all these superstitious beliefs in Arab society were eliminated. In *Surah al-Ra'd* it states:

> *Allah is He Who raised the heavens without any pillars, that you can see.* (13:2)

Thus, in a single throw, this verse invalidated the belief that the sky remains above simply because of the mountains. In many other subjects, too, important facts were revealed at a time when no one could have known anything about them.

CRUCIAL ASPECTS OF THE QUR'ĀN

- The Qur'ān's principal objective is to form a righteous man and establish a virtuous community.
- The Qur'ān is not a book of astrology, nor of medicine.
- The Qur'ān's words need not reflect the norms of the present time, nor do they necessarily share connotations with recent theories and knowledge.
- The Qur'ān's words are very well-contrived and accurate, as they are composed by Allah, Who has perfected everything.

The Qur'ān's purpose behind delivering medical and scientific references, and other miracles are numerous, of which the most significant are that it reinforces and strengthens Muslims' faith by motivating them towards admonition, deliberation and meditation. It also provides non-Muslims with conclusive evidence of Islam's genuineness. The Prophet Muḥammad (peace be upon him), himself, was not familiar with such scientific issues as have only been revealed in recent decades, unless he was told of these by Allah the Almighty:

> *Soon will We show them Our signs in the (furthest) regions (of the earth), and in their own souls, until it becomes manifest to them that this is the Truth.* (41:53)

Let us take for example this verse:

> *O mankind! If you have a doubt about the Resurrection.* (22:5)

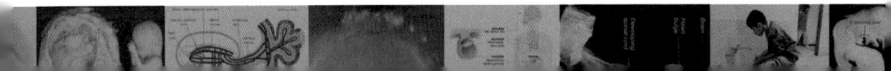

and here is the evidence:

We created you out of dust, then out of a sperm, then out of a leech-like clot, then out of a morsel of flesh, partly formed and partly unformed, in order that We might make clear Our signs; and We cause whom We will to rest in the wombs for an appointed term, then do We bring you out as babes, then (foster you) that you may reach your age of full strength; and some of you are called to die, and some are sent back to the feeblest old age, so that they know nothing." (22:5)

The verse goes on:

And you see the earth barren, but when We pour down rain on it, it is stirred (to life), it swells and it puts forth every kind of beautiful growth in pairs. (22:5)

The Qur'ān encourages all that helps reveal the secrets of the universe and existence. It is also the Qur'ān that strengthens one's faith in Allah:

Say: 'Travel through the earth and see how Allah did originate creation; so will Allah produce a later creation: for Allah has power over all things. (29:20)

Now, let us take a closer look at some of these medical miracles revealed in the Qur'ān.

Chapter 1

Embryology and Human Creation: The Qur'ān and Science

HISTORICAL BACKGROUND

Although Aristotle summed up the prevailing theories of his age relating to the creation of the embryo, controversy continued among the supporters of different theories. Briefly, followers fell into two camps, those who argued that the full dwarf embryo existed in man's sperm and those who argued that the full dwarf embryo was created out of the woman's menstrual blood coagulation (thickening). Most believed that man was reduced into that sperm drop, and they drew a figure in which they imagined the embryo as a full creature in the sperm drop, which then developed in the womb as a small tree, (see Figure 1).

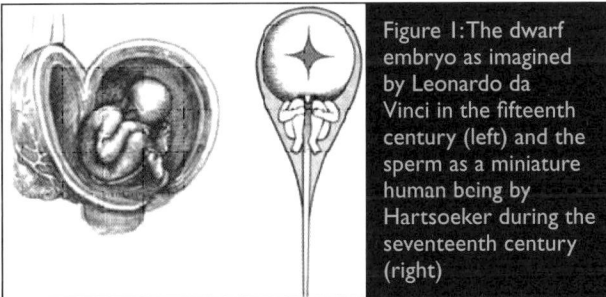

Figure 1: The dwarf embryo as imagined by Leonardo da Vinci in the fifteenth century (left) and the sperm as a miniature human being by Hartsoeker during the seventeenth century (right)

Neither group realized that man's sperm and woman's ovum participate in the creation of the embryo, as supported by the Italian scientist Spallanzani in 1775. In 1783, Van Beneden was able to confirm this statement, and thus the idea of the dwarf embryo was discarded. During the years 1888 and 1909 Boveri proved that chromosomes, when divided, carry the different genetic characteristics of each individual. Morgan, in 1912, was able to determine the role of genes, existing in certain parts of chromosomes, in a hereditary continuum.

Therefore, it is clear that mankind did not realize until the eighteenth century that the embryo is created of a man's sperm mingled with a woman's ovum. Furthermore, this was only confirmed at the beginning of the twentieth century.

On the other hand, the Holy Qur'ān and the Prophetic speeches confirmed in a very accurate scientific manner the creation of man from a mingled fluid-drop (*nuṭfa amshāj*). As the Qur'ān states:

> *Verily We created man from a drop of mingled sperm* (nuṭfa amshāj), *in order to try him: so We gave him (the gifts), of hearing and sight* (76:2)

It has been agreed upon by commentators of the Holy Qur'ān that *amshāj* means mingling, as man's water mingles with that of the woman and this is also what the Prophet confirmed in one of his speeches. Imām Aḥmad indicated in his book *Al-Musnad* that a Jew passed by Prophet Muḥammad (peace be upon him) while he was addressing his companions. Some of the Quraysh responded by saying:

"O Jew! This man proclaims that he is a prophet."
The Jew said: "I will ask him of something no one
knows except a prophet." He asked the Prophet:
"O Muḥammad! What is man created from?" The
Prophet said: "O Jew! Man is created from both: man's
fluid (**nutfa**) and woman's fluid." The Jew said: "This is
what was said by those prophets before you."

In the next few pages, the embryological developments
as indicated in the Qur'ānic verses will be discussed. We
will also shed light on the fixed scientific facts in each stage
of development.

SPERM

Sperm are formed in the testicles, which in turn are
created, as proved by embryology, from cells underneath
the kidneys at the back, which then go down to the lower
abdomen during the last weeks of pregnancy. Man's fluid
mainly consists of the following components: the sperm
which should be gushing and motile to cause fertilization
and prostaglandin which causes contractions to the
uterus, thus helping the transportation of sperm into the
place of fertilization. The man's fluid (semen) also contains
sugar, necessary for the provision of energy to the sperm,
different fluids for neutralising the acids at the entrance
of the uterus and creating a slippery environment for the
easy movement of the sperm.

While hundreds of millions of these sperm, 500-600
million, enter through the vagina to the uterine cervix,
only one sperm is able to fertilize the ovum (see Figure 2),
crossing a long distance to reach the place of fertilization

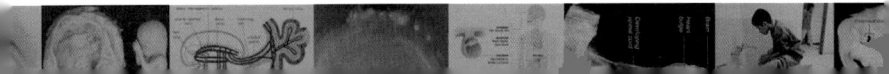

in the fallopian uterine tube which connects the ovary with the uterus. This distance is full of obstacles that can be compared with the enormous efforts man takes to reach the moon! After direct fertilization, a quick change occurs to the membrane of the ovum preventing entrance of the remaining sperm.

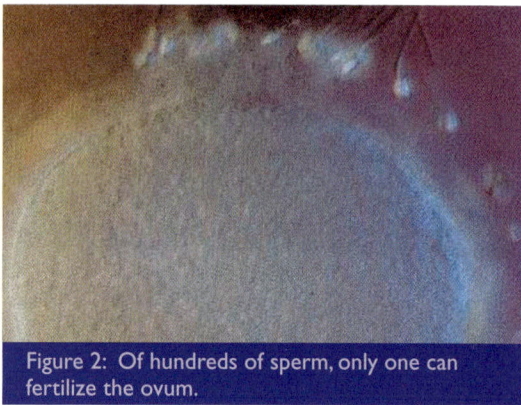

Figure 2: Of hundreds of sperm, only one can fertilize the ovum.

The sperm contains 23 chromosomes, of which one chromosome determines the sex of the embryo. The chromosome in the sperm is either (Y) or (X), while the chromosome in the ovum is always (X). When a sperm of chromosome type (Y) mingles with an ovum of chromosome (X), the formed zygote will be male (XY), whereas the embryo will be female (XX) if sperm (X) mingles with an (X) ovum. So, the sex of the embryo is determined by the sperm (the male), rather than the ovum (the female).

After five hours of forming the zygote, which is the primary human cell containing 46 chromosomes, dominant and recessive genetic characteristics can appear (the

stage of genetic programming). The zygote is then divided quickly (see Figure 3) without any change in size and then moves from the fallopian tube (connecting the ovary and the uterus) towards the uterus, where it is implanted as seeds are implanted in soil.

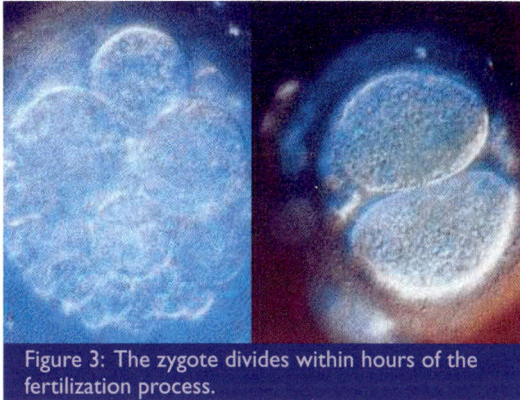

Figure 3: The zygote divides within hours of the fertilization process.

The uterus is the place where the embryo grows and develops before emerging as a fully created and well formed child. The uterus is distinguished as a safe place to perform this function for the following reasons:

1. The location of the uterus is in the woman's pelvis, where it is protected with ligaments and fascia that hold the uterus from the sides and allow its mobility and growth to a hundred times its size at full term pregnancy.

2. The muscles of the pelvis and perineum fix the uterus *in-situ*.

3. The secretion of progesterone (pregnancy hormone) helps stabilize the uterus and slows down the uterine contractions.

4. The embryo in the uterus is surrounded with different membranes that produce amniotic fluid, which the embryo swims in to protect itself from the effect of external trauma.

The process of fertilization and the zygote's travel to the uterus continue for about six days, and the zygote keeps implanting (this is known as blastocyst) and growing in the uterus wall for fifteen days, when the *'alaqa* (thick clotted blood) stage begins.

Reflections on the Qur'ān and Sunnah

Nuṭfa in Arabic means 'very little water' or 'a drop of water'. This coincides with man's water which contains sperm as part of its components. The sperm or (spermatozoon) is reproduced from the despised lowly water (*nuṭfa*) and looks like a long-tailed fish (this is one of the meanings of sulalah). Allah the Almighty says:

> He Who has made everything which He has created most good: he began the creation of man with nothing more than clay, and made his progeny from an extract of despised fluid (sulālah)." (32:7-8)

The other meaning of **sulālah** is 'extract', in other words the essential or best part of something. By either implication, it means 'part of a whole' indicating that the origin of creation is from only part of man's fluid and not all of it (which contains many components as shown above). Clarifying the role of **nuṭfa** in creation, He, the Almighty, says:

Now, let man think from what he is created! He is created from a drop emitted." (86:5-6)

Furthermore, He says:

He has created man from a sperm-drop and behold this same (man) becomes an open disputer!" (16:4)

The Qur'ān tells us also that the essence of man is not the whole semen, but only a small part of it. This is explained in the Qur'ān as follows:

Does man think that he will be left uncontrolled (without purpose)? Was he not once a drop of sperm emitted (in lowly form)?" (75:36-37)

As we have seen, the Qur'ān informs us that man is made not from the entire semen, but only a small part of it. That the particular emphasis in this statement announces a fact only discovered by modern science is evidence that the statement is divine in origin. The divine statement also reiterates that man's characteristics are determined and decreed in the **nuṭfa** stage. As He says:

Woe to man! What has made him reject Allah? From what stuff has He created him? From a nuṭfa (sperm-drop) He has created him, and then moulds him in due proportions." (80:17-19)

And Allah says:

Verily We created man from a drop (nutfa), of mingled sperm (amshaj), in order to try him: so We gave him (the gifts) of hearing and sight." (76:2)

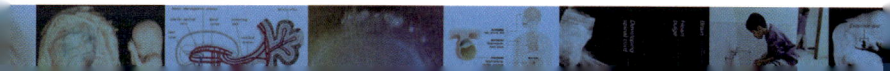

The mingled *nuṭfa* in this verse reveals the Qur'ān's miraculous nature. *Nuṭfa*, in Arabic, is a single, small drop of water, but it was described here as *amshāj*, which means its structure consists of combined mixtures. This fits with scientific findings, as the zygote is shaped as a drop, and is simultaneously a mixture of male fluid chromosomes and female ovum chromosomes.

Before the Qur'ān was revealed did anyone ever think that man's *nuṭfa*, when ejected, is responsible for determining whether the embryo is male or female? Did this ever occur to anyone? The Qur'ān says:

> *That He did create in pairs, male and female, from a seed when lodged (in its place)."* (53:45-46)

This confirms that man's gender as male or female is determined when that drop of sperm is emitted. Who told the Prophet Muḥammad (peace be upon him) that the sperm *(nuṭfa)* bearing one of its types, (Y) or (X) is responsible for determining the sex of the embryo? Such distinctions were not made until after the invention of microscopes; it was only then that it became apparent that gender was determined by the sperm *(nuṭfa)*, rather than the ovum. In other words, even during the early twentieth century mankind was ignorant about the fact that the *nuṭfa* decrees if the embryo is male or female. Conversely, the Qur'ān, which was revealed 14 centuries ago, stated this fact in a very clear manner.

We mentioned earlier that sperm are formed in the testicles, which in turn are created, as proved by embryology, from cells underneath the kidneys at the back and which then go down to the lower abdomen

during the last weeks of pregnancy. This is in confirmation of Allah's saying:

> *And when your Lord brought forth from the children of Adam, from their loins, their descendants."* (7:172)

This is a clear indication that the origin of progeny is in the region of the back where the embryonic testicles are formed. So, praise be to Allah the Omniscient.

The uterus, as mentioned before, is considered as a place settled (***makīn***), somewhere as we stated earlier safe for the embryo's growth and protection. We find that the Qur'ān mentioned and affirmed this fact 14 centuries ago, when He, the Almighty, said:

> *That which (embryo) We placed in a place of rest, firmly fixed for a period (of gestation), determined. For We do determine, for We are the best to determine (things).* (77:21-23)

AL-'ALAQA (LEECH-LIKE CLOT)

The stage of '*alaqa* starts on Day 15 and ends on Day 23 or 24, after which the embryo is gradually developed and looks like a pond-living leech, (see Figure 4). '*Alaqa* hangs to the lining of the uterus by the umbilical cord. Blood is then formed in the vessels in the shape of closed islands. It is not circulated in blood vessels, and thus has the appearance of clotted blood.

Although it is in the nature of the human body to expel any external matter, the uterus does not reject the '*alaqa* implanted in its lining despite the fact that half of the '*alaqa's* components and genes emanate from an

external source (the father). This is because the region of syncytial cells in *'alaqa* contain no antigens.

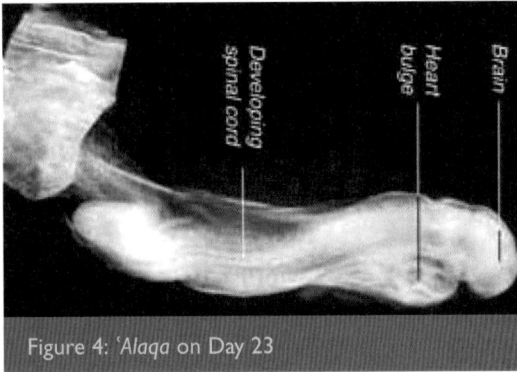

Figure 4: *'Alaqa* on Day 23

It is noteworthy that the primitive streak is first created on Day 14 or 15, in which the primitive node appears (see Figure 5). Out of this primitive streak, stem cells are composed, as well as the sources of the main tissues – mesoderm, ectoderm and endoderm – which form the different organs and tissues of the body as seen in (Figure 6). At the end of the 3rd week, this primitive streak shrinks and the remnant stays in the sacrococcygeal region at the end of the spine, maintaining the remaining stem cells in this region. This explains why some tumours in the coccygeal region which is called **teratoma** (see Figure 7) can contain different tissues (muscles, skin, cartilage, bones and teeth as well), contrary to those tumours that exist in different regions and take their toll on one definite tissue.

Prechordal plate
Oropharyngeal membrane
Neural fold
Cranial end
Embryonic ectoderm
Neural plate
Primitive node
Notochordal process
Primitive streak
Newly added cells
Caudal end
Cloacal membrane
Notochord deep to neural groove

A 15 days   **B** 17 days   **C** 18 days   **D** 21 days

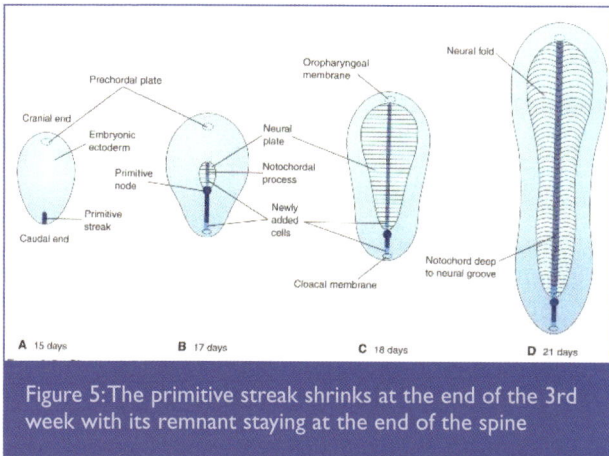

Figure 5: The primitive streak shrinks at the end of the 3rd week with its remnant staying at the end of the spine

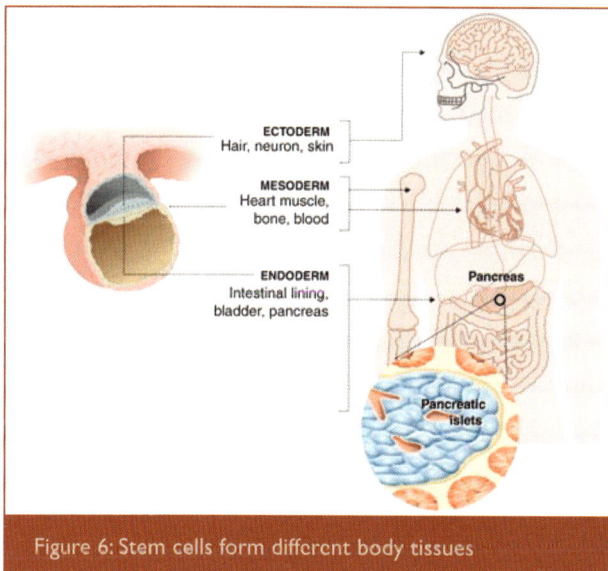

ECTODERM
Hair, neuron, skin

MESODERM
Heart muscle, bone, blood

ENDODERM
Intestinal lining, bladder, pancreas

Pancreas

Pancreatic islets

Figure 6: Stem cells form different body tissues

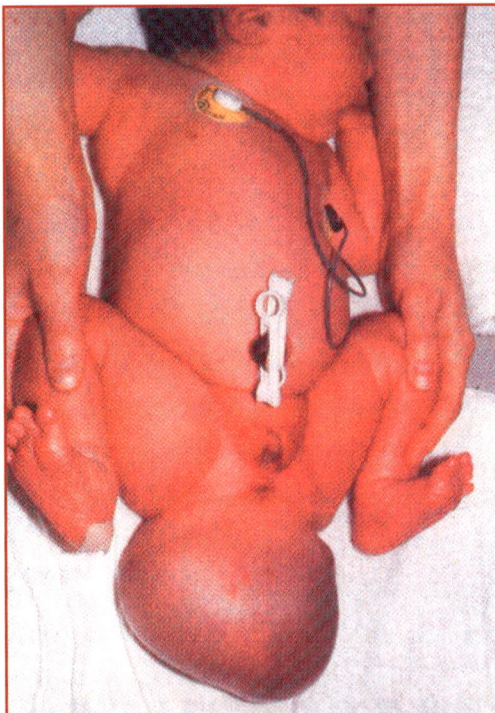

Figure 7: *Teratoma* in the coccygeal region at the end of the spine in a female infant

Reflections on the Qur'ān and Sunnah

The transformation process from *nuṭfa* to *ʿalaqa* takes more than ten days until the zygote clings to the primitive placenta by way of a connecting stalk which later becomes the umbilical cord. Therefore, the Qur'ānic statement uses the Arabic conjunctive *thumma* (in Arabic) indicating the sequence of events with a time delay and so avoids using *fa* (in Arabic) which also means 'then' but which indicates rapid progression without any delay. The Qur'ān states:

> *Then of that fluid-drop (nuṭfa) We created a leech-like clot."* (23:14)

ʿAlaqa, in Arabic, possesses several different meanings:
• A leech that lives in ponds and sucks the blood of other creatures.
• A thing attached or clinging to something else.
• Clotted or coagulated blood.

All these meanings fit exactly with the reality of the human embryo after its implantation in the lining of the uterus (endometrium). The embryo, resembling a leech, as shown in Figure 8, clings to the endometrium through the umbilical cord (Figure 9), and blood vessels initiated in the form of closed islands giving it the appearance of clotted blood (see Figure 10).

A quick transformation then occurs from *ʿalaqa* to *muḍgha* within two days (Day 24 to Day 26). Therefore, the Qur'ān describes this rapid change by using the conjunctive article *fa*, i.e. 'then' (in Arabic) to indicate rapid progression and transformation:

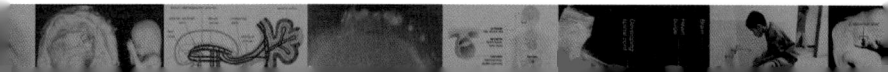

> *Then We changed the ʿAlaqa (leech-like clot) into a muġḍha (chewed-like lump).* (23:14)

So even the use of different conjunctive articles carry miraculous indications, reflecting the difference in embryonic stages.

Thus, *ʿalaqa* is the second embryonic stage, and it is mentioned in the Qur'ān in several verses. He, the Almighty, says:

> *Was he not a drop of sperm emitted (in lowly form)? Then did he become a leech-like clot; then did (Allah) make and fashion (him) in due proportion. And of him He made two sexes, male and female.* (75:37-39)

And in a *surah* called **al-ʿAlaq** i.e. a leech-like clot, Allah says:

> *(We) created man, out of a (mere) clot of congealed blood.* (96:2)

The primitive streak is the first to be created in embryo, and out of this stem cells are composed, as well as the different organs and tissues. At the end of the 3rd week, it shrinks but stays in the sacrococcygeal region at the end of the spine, maintaining the remaining stem cells in this region. This explains and coincides with the Prophet's speech, which was narrated by Abū Hurayra in Aḥmad's book **Al-Musnad**:

> All of the son of Adam decays, and is eaten by dust except for the coccyx, of which man is created and in which man is re-built.

A. Human Embryo

cut edge of amnion

forebrain

heart

B. Leech

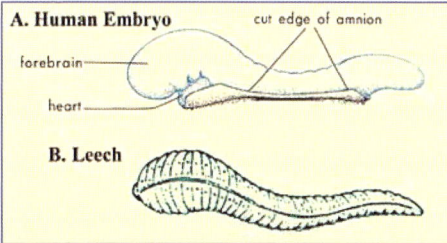

Figure 8: Illustration of an embryo (top) that looks like a leech (bottom)

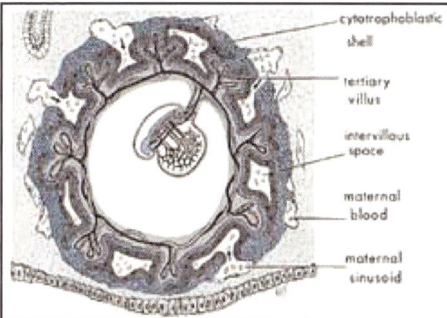

cytotrophoblastic shell

tertiary villus

intervillous space

maternal blood

maternal sinusoid

Figure 9: An embryo clinging to the lining of the uterus through the umbilical

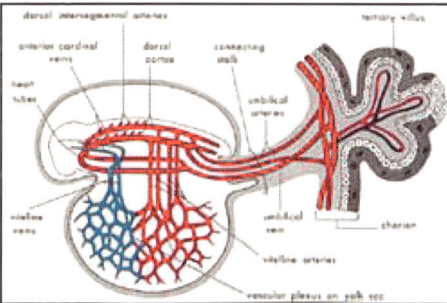

dorsal intersegmental arteries

anterior cardinal veins

dorsal aortae

connecting stalk

heart tubes

umbilical arteries

tertiary villus

vitelline veins

umbilical vein

chorion

vitelline arteries

vascular plexus on yolk sac

Figure 10: The closed blood vessel net causing the embryo to look like clotted blood.

So, cells which form man's tissues and organs are placed in the coccyx. Verily, this is what Allah's Prophet said. Here a very important question arises: why did the Prophet Muḥammad (peace be upon him) raise such a scientific issue at a time when no one was aware of, let alone how he acquired such knowledge unless he were bound with inspiration and taught by the Creator of heaven and earth? The answer is that Allah the Almighty knows with His encompassing knowledge that man will one day come to know the embryonic stages of development, and will know the role of the primitive streak. Hence, He inspired Prophet Muḥammad (peace be upon him) to speak about this fact such that this could bear witness to the genuineness of his prophethood and message.

AL-MUḌGHA (A CHEWED-LIKE LUMP OF FLESH)

The embryo is transformed from the stage of ʿalaqa to that of the beginning of **muḍgha** on Day 24 -26. This is a very brief period when compared with the **nuṭfa** changing to the ʿalaqa.

This stage starts with the appearance of somites on Day 24 or 25 on top of the embryonic scapula, and which then gradually appear at the embryo's buttocks. On Day 28 the embryo is formed of several bulges, with grooves in between, thus giving the embryo the image of chewed gum. The embryo turns and rolls in the cavity of the uterus during this stage which is complete by the end of the 6th week. (See Figure 11)

It is noteworthy that the **muḍgha** stage starts with the growth and increase of cells in large number. The **muḍgha** looks like a piece of meat which has no distinguished

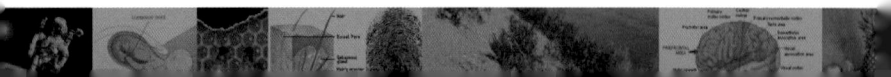

structure, then after a few days, the second stage starts, called the formation *(takhalluq)*, where some organs begin to appear, such as the eyes, tongue and lips, but human distinguishing features do not appear until the end of the 8th week. Limb bulges (hands and legs) also appear in this stage.

In the 5th week, the heart starts beating and the embryo has already developed its placenta and amniotic sac. The placenta is burrowing into the uterine wall to access oxygen and nutrients from the mother's bloodstream.

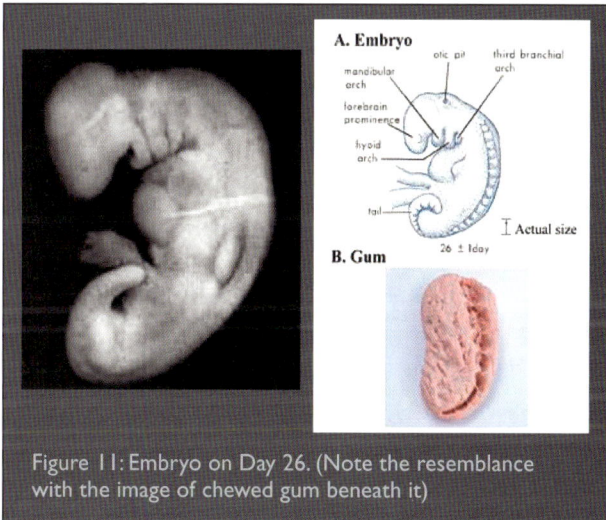

Figure 11: Embryo on Day 26. (Note the resemblance with the image of chewed gum beneath it)

Reflections on the Qur'ān and Sunna

Muḍgha in Arabic means the material chewed by teeth. This gives an accurate description of the embryonic stage as the embryo shape looks like chewed material which constantly changes, and which has the appearance of somite bulges. The differences in these somites look like 'teeth imprints' on bitten bread. The embryo turns and rolls in the cavity of the uterus just as does a piece of chewed material in the mouth. *Muḍgha* comes after the *ʿalaqa* stage. This also coincides with the verse:

> *Then of that clot We made a (foetus) lump.* (23:14)

One of the characteristics of **muḍgha** is that it elongates and changes shape when chewed. This is exactly what occurs to the embryo during this stage. As we mentioned earlier, the **muḍgha** has an early form before the creation and formation of organs and another form following the formation of organs. The relevant Qur'ānic verse states:

> *O mankind! If you have a doubt about the Resurrection (consider) that We created you out of dust, then out of sperm, then out of a leech-like clot, then out of a chewed-like lump, partly formed and partly unformed, in order that We might manifest (Our power) to you; and We cause whom We will to rest in the wombs for an appointed term."* (22:5)

Thus, there are two types of **muḍgha**: formed and unformed. The formed is the embryo itself, which starts growing into different organs with specific functions. The unformed one is the placenta, which starts developing in the 5th week (around Day 35) of the **muḍgha** stage. And Allah knows best!

The **muḍgha** stage ends at the 6th week (i.e. Day 40). Imām Muslim narrated in his Ṣaḥīḥ on the authority of ʿAbdullāh bin Masʿūd that: Allah's Prophet Muḥammad (peace be upon him) – the truthful and trustworthy – told us:

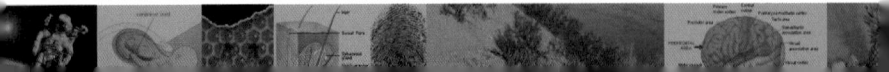

The creation of each one of you is composed in the mother's womb in forty days, in that (creation) it turns into such a *'alaqa* (clot) in that it turns into such a **muḍgha** and then Allah sends an angel and orders him to write four things, i.e., his provision, his age, and whether he will be of the wretched or the blessed (in the Hereafter). Then the soul is breathed into him. And by Allah, a person among you (or a man) may do deeds of the people of the Fire till there is only a cubit or an arms-breadth between him and the Fire, but then that writing (which Allah has ordered the angel to write) precedes, and he does the deeds of the people of Paradise and enters it; and a man may do the deeds of the people of Paradise till there is only a cubit or two between him and Paradise, and then that writing precedes and he does the deeds of the people of the Fire and enters it.

Who told the Prophet Muḥammad (peace be upon him) all these facts? Did he have anatomy and measurement tools, or microscopes to tell us the characteristics of an embryo no more than one centimetre tall? No, it is rather He, Allah, (Who told him), the Only One, the Subduer.

THE BONE STAGE

During the 6th week, the cartilaginous skeleton starts to spread in the body (see Figure 12). Yet, we do not see the human features until the beginning of the 7th week (see Figure 13), where the shape of the embryo takes on the look of a skeleton. This transformation from the

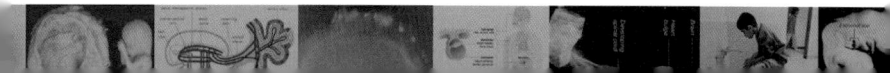

muḍgha to the beginning of a skeleton occurs in a very short period of time at the end of the 6th week and the beginning of the 7th week. This stage is characterized by the appearance of a skeleton which gives the embryo human characteristics.

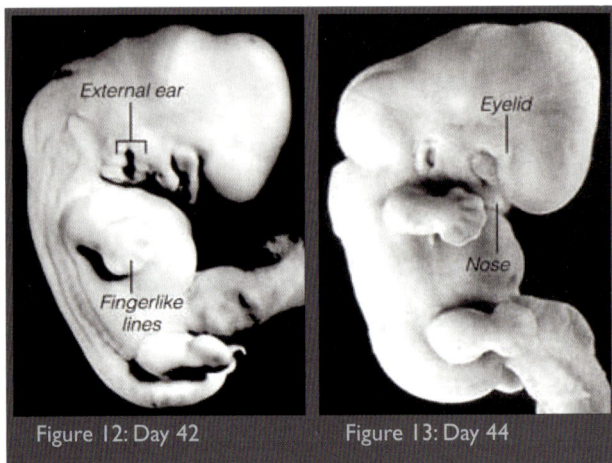

Figure 12: Day 42   Figure 13: Day 44

Reflections on the Qur'ān and Sunnah

The term *iẓām* (bones), coined by the Qur'ān, accurately expresses this stage in the embryo's life. This is when external appearance commences and it is considered the most important change in the internal structure, with its associated new relations among body organs and the regularity of embryo shape. This stage is clearly distinguished from the preceding *muḍgha* (chewed-like lump of flesh) stage. Allah says:

> We made that lump (muḍgha), bones, and clothed the bones with flesh; then We developed out of it another creature. So blessed be Allah, the best to create!" (23:14)

Because of the very short time duration during which this transformation takes place, the Qur'ānic verse uses the Arabic conjunctive article **fa** instead of **thumma** to indicate its quick sequence of events. This skeleton gives the embryo the image of a human being after being clothed with **laḥm** (muscles). The two eyes and the two lips then appear, and the head is differentiated from the trunk and the limbs. This is in accordance with the Prophet's statement recorded in **Ṣaḥīḥ Muslim**:

> When 42 nights have passed over the conception, Allah sends an angel to it, who shapes it (into human form) and makes its ears, eyes, skin, muscles and bones. Then he says: 'O Lord, is it male or female?' and your Lord decides what He wishes and the angel records it.

After 42 nights (6 weeks), the embryo begins to take on a human image with the appearance of the cartilaginous skeleton, then the external genitals appear later on, during the 10th week. In the 7th week (see Figure 13) these human characteristics become clearer with the start of the skeleton's spread. This week represents Day 40-45, the demarcation line between **muḍgha** and human. Hence, it is well proved that the Qur'ān's words are very well contrived and scientifically accurate. No wonder: they are composed by Allah Who has perfected everything.

THE MUSCLE STAGE (CLOTHING WITH FLESH)

This stage is characterized with muscles encircling and tightly surrounding the bones. With this clothing of the bones with **laḥm** (muscles and flesh), the human starts

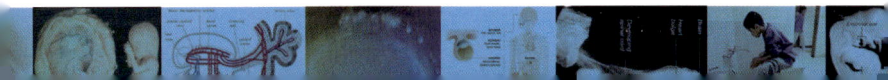

to become clearer, as human parts are appropriately connected. After completion of myogenesis (muscle formation), the embryo can then start to move. This stage, which starts at the end of the 7th week (see Figure 14) and finishes at the end of the 8th week (see Figure 15), is considered to conclude the **takhalluq** (formation) stage. Embryologists term the end of the 8th week as the last of the embryological stage followed by the foetal stage which coincides with the **nash'a** (developing) stage as stated by the Qur'ān:

> *And clothed the bones with flesh; then We developed out of it another creature. So blessed be Allah, the best to create!* (23:14)

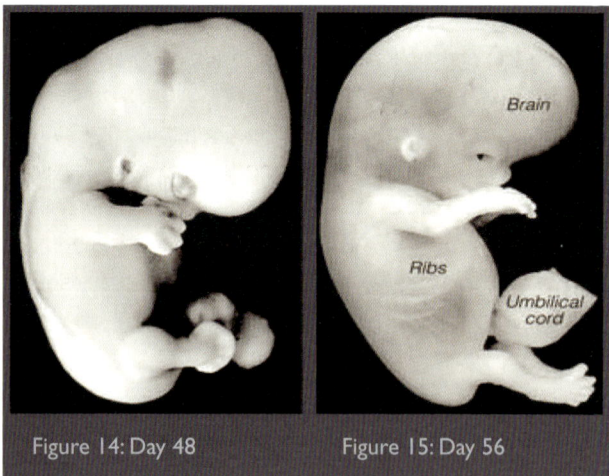

Figure 14: Day 48   Figure 15: Day 56

Until very recently, embryologists assumed that the bones and muscles in an embryo developed at the

same time. For this reason, for a long time, some people claimed that these verses conflicted with science. Yet, advanced microscopic research conducted by virtue of new technological developments has revealed that the revelation of the Qur'ān is word for word correct. These observations at the microscopic level showed that the development inside the mother's womb takes place in just the way it is described in the holy book. First, the cartilage tissue of the embryo ossifies. Then muscular cells that are selected from amongst the tissue around the bones come together and wrap around the bones

THE *NASH'A* (DEVELOPING) STAGE AND VIABILITY

By the end of the 8th week, a new stage starts where important processes occur. The rate of development accelerates as compared with the previous one. The embryo transforms into another creature, as the sizes of head, body and limbs start to be balanced and regular between the 9th and 12th week. At the 10th week, external genital organs appear, and the skeleton develops structure from soft cartilaginous to hard calcic bones at the 12th week (Figure 16). Limbs and fingers are distinguished at the same week. The gender of the embryo is manifest with the clear appearance of genitalia.

The weight of the embryo increases noticeably. Voluntary and involuntary muscles develop, and voluntary movements start in this stage. In the 16th week (Day 112) the foetus can grasp with its hands, kick, or even somersault (Figure 17).

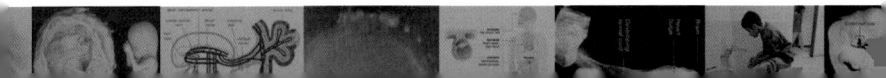

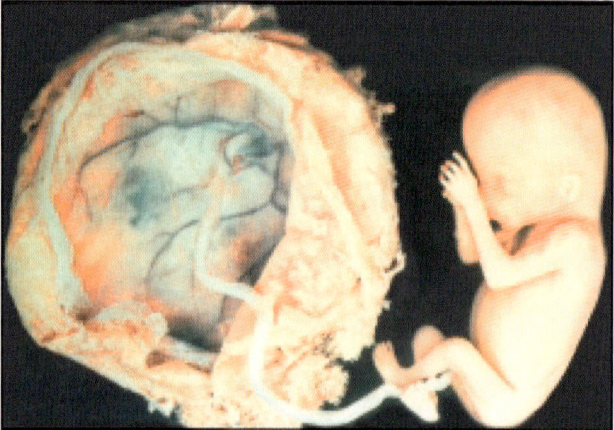

Figure 16: The 12th week (around Day 84). The embryonic shape appears with the head, body and limbs well formed, and fingers distinguished. (*Nash'ah* equates with the 'formation of another creature')

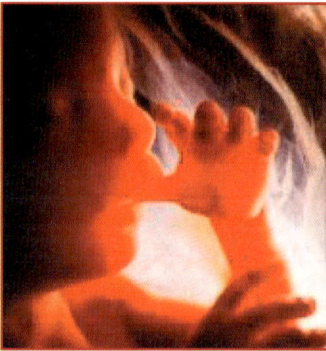

Figure 17: The 16th week (Day 112). A 13 cm tall embryo; eyebrows, eyelashes and fine hair appear. The foetus can grasp with its hands, kick, or even somersault. Here the unborn baby is sucking its thumb!

In this stage, the organs and other systems prepare to function. The foetus is ready for life outside the womb starting from the 22nd to the 26th week (i.e. after completion of the 6th month of gestation), when the respiratory system is ready to function and the nervous

system is able to adjust the temperature of the foetus body.

The first sense to develop in a human embryo is hearing. The foetus can hear sounds after the 24th week. Subsequently, sight is developed and by the 28th week the retina becomes sensitive to light. In this stage, no new system or organs are formed, and the uterus provides food and a suitable environment for the foetus to thrive until the labour stage.

Reflections on the Qur'ān and Sunna

This stage starts after clothing the bones with *laḥm* (muscles and flesh), i.e., at the beginning of the 9th week, and takes almost 3 weeks. This is indicated by use of the conjunctive article *thumma*, 'then', which denotes a time break between clothing with *laḥm* and developing into another creature. He, the Almighty, says:

> *And clothed the bones with flesh; then We developed out of it another creature. So blessed be Allah, the best to create!* (23:14)

After the development of the cartilaginous skeleton, clothing it with muscles, and the distinguishing of the head and the limbs, the embryo changes into a human creature well differentiated from other creatures. During this stage, some important processes occur in the embryo's development, which are clearly described in the Qur'ān and can be summarized as follows:

1. *Nash'a* (developing), which is clearly noticed in the accelerated rate of growth at the 9th week compared with the previous stages.

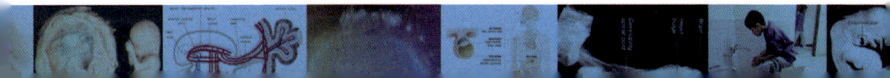

2. *Khalqan ākhar* (another creature). This description coincides with the first one and indicates that the embryo has changed in the *nash'a* stage into another creature, i.e.,the foetus. Limbs and external organs begin to appear, and fingers and external genitalia are distinguished. Allah the Almighty says:

> *He it is Who shapes you in the wombs as He pleases. There is no god but He, the Exalted in Might, the Wise.* (3:6)

In *Sūrah al-Zumar* Allah provides us with an exquisite remark:

> *He makes you in the wombs of your mothers in stages, one after another, in three veils of darkness.* (39:6)

This, thus, indicates the continuation of the embryonic development and the change from one stage into another, as explained earlier. Embryologists have confirmed that the foetus is surrounded, during the stages of development, with three membranes:

1. The amnion membrane which contains a fluid encompassing the foetus to enable it to swim, thus protecting it from any trauma the uterus encounters. This also facilitates the foetal movements for smooth re-positioning during labour. (see Figure 18.)
2. The chorion membrane.
3. The decidua membrane.

Some scholars have interpreted the three veils of darkness with the amniotic membrane surrounding the uterus, the uterus wall, and abdomen wall (see Figure 19). Yet, Allah knows best!

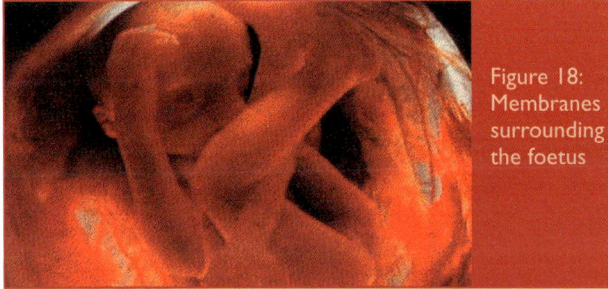

Figure 18: Membranes surrounding the foetus

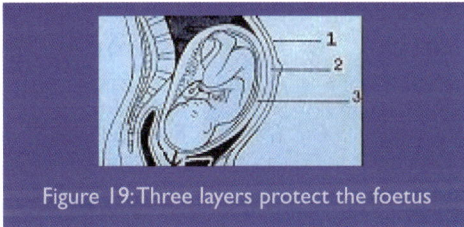

Figure 19: Three layers protect the foetus

As we have already mentioned, the foetus becomes ready for life outside the womb after completion of the 6th month. It is worth noting that the Qur'ānic statement in *Sūrah al-Aḥqāf* indicates that the stage of conception and incubation takes 30 months:

> *The carrying of (the child) and the weaning is (a period of) thirty months.* (46:15)

In *Sūrah Luqmān*, however, the period of incubation is described as 24 months:

> *And in two years was his weaning.* (31:14)

With a simple calculation, we can deduce that the Qur'ānic statement decides that the least period of conception is 6 months, now a scientific fact, and before the 22nd week the foetus is delivered **abortus** (unable to survive) in most cases. Praise be to Allah, the Omniscient.

It is very interesting to note that the first sense to develop in a human embryo is hearing. The foetus can hear sounds after the 24th week. Subsequently, sight is developed and by the 28th week, the retina becomes sensitive to light. Consider the following three Quranic verses relating to the development of senses in the embryo:

> *And He gave you (the faculties of) hearing and sight and feeling (And understanding).* (32:9)
>
> *Verily We created man from a drop of a mingled sperm* (nuṭfa amshāj), *in order to try him: so We gave him (the gifts), of hearing and sight.* (76:2)
>
> *It is He Who has created for you (the faculties of) hearing, sight, feeling and understanding: little thanks it is you give!* (23:78)

In all three verses the sense of hearing is mentioned before the sense of sight. Thus the Qur'ānic description matches with the discoveries of modern embryology.

THE LABOUR STAGE

After the passing of 9 lunar months (38 weeks), the foetus completes its growth in the uterus. It is time now to leave after the end of this specified period. Allah says:

> *And We cause whom We will to rest in the wombs for an appointed term.* (22:5)

So the term is appointed and determined:

> *That (foetus) which We placed in a place of rest, firmly fixed, for a period (of gestation), determined (according to need). For We do determine, for We are the best to determine (things).* (77: 21-23)

Before elaborating upon the stages of labour, it is worth noting that the Qur'ān refers to the benefits of dates for women in labour. This is made in reference to Mary, mother of the Prophet 'Isa:

> *And the pains of child birth drove her to the trunk of a palm tree: she cried: 'Ah! would that I had died before this! would that I had been a thing forgotten and out of sight.' But (a voice) cried to her from beneath the palm tree: 'Grieve not! For your Lord has set below you a rivulet. Shake towards yourself the trunk of the palm tree, it will let fall fresh ripe dates upon you. So eat, and drink, and be comforted."* (19:23-26)

It has been scientifically proven that dates provide several benefits. Of these the following are specifically good for women in labour:

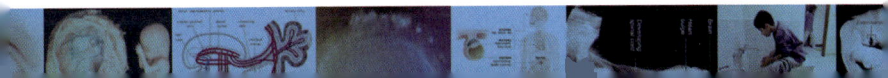

1. Dates are rich in fibre which help avoid constipation. They are, thus, a natural laxative, and help with smooth delivery.
2. Dates contain more than 70% glucose, which is easily absorbed and assimilated, thus ensuring the provision of necessary energy during labour.
3. Dates are also rich in minerals, particularly magnesium which is necessary for cell physiology, potassium for the muscles, and iron with which to treat anemia.
4. Dates contain a substance that helps alert the muscles of the uterus to contract and increase contraction during delivery (this substance resembles the oxytocin hormone excreted by the pituitary glands).

Labour, which ends with delivery, is comprised of 4 stages:
1. Dilatation of the cervix and contraction of the uterus muscle. This stage takes about 7-12 hours (see Figure 20) and occurs as a result of several factors: mechanic and hormonal. A set of hormones is excreted to help facilitate the labour stage. Among these hormones are prostaglandin, corticotropin releasing hormone, adreno cortico tropin, corticol, oxytocin, and oestrogen.
2. Delivering the foetus. This stage takes about 30-50 minutes, and starts after sufficient dilatation of the cervix. As a result of consequent uterus contractions, the foetus head starts to emerge first (see Figure 21). It is striking that the diameter of the foetus head may exceed 12 cm i.e., normally triple the diameter of the vaginal canal. Having considered this fact, and the role of self hormonal factors, in addition to the expansion

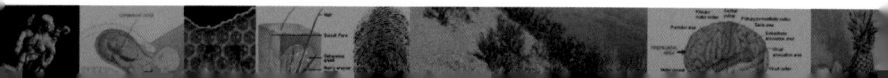

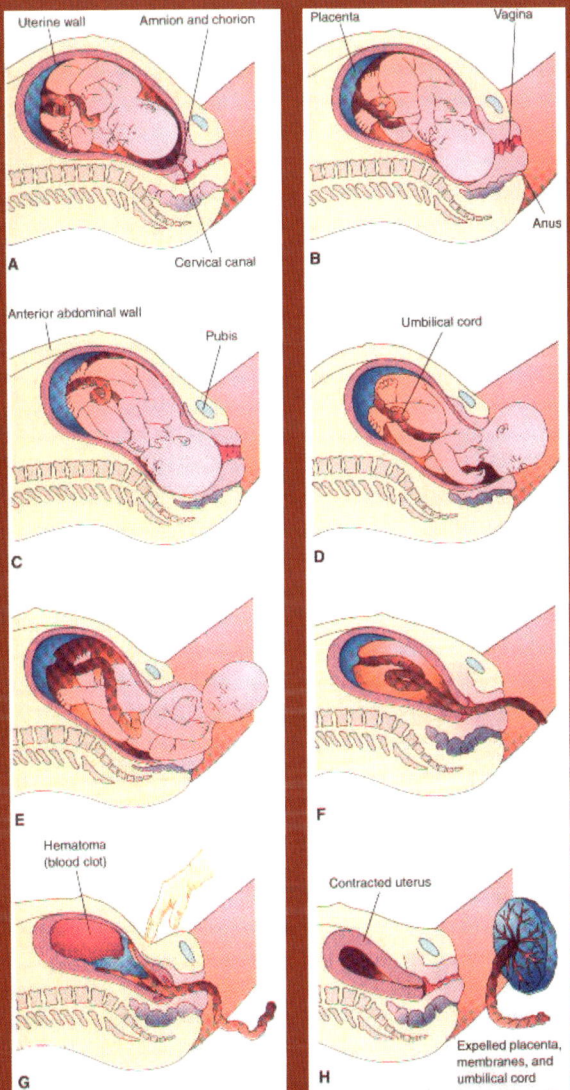

Figure 20: The stages of labour

of pelvis ligatures and muscles, that all facilitate the delivery of the foetus, we realize the wisdom underlying Allah's saying:

Then does He makes his path smooth for him. (80:20)

Blessed be Allah, the Most Wise of all disposers.

3. Emergence of the placenta and the formation of a blood clot behind the placenta (see Figure 19). This stage lasts about 15 minutes.

4. Uterus contraction. This is to alleviate bleeding after the delivery process, and continues for about two hours.

After delivery, and cutting the umbilical cord (see Figure 22), which the foetus has depended upon for acquiring food from its mother during pregnancy, the baby then starts another stage in a new station of its life.

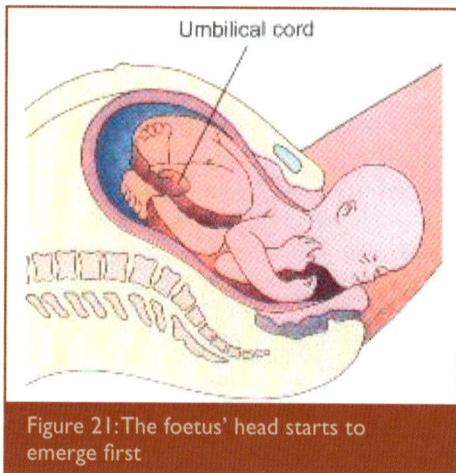

Umbilical cord

Figure 21: The foetus' head starts to emerge first

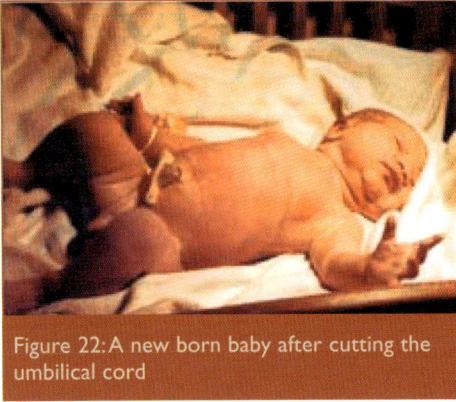

Figure 22: A new born baby after cutting the umbilical cord

CONCLUSION

The miracle of human creation in the Holy Qur'ān is one of many other medical miracles. Having reviewed many Qur'ānic verses and scientific analysis of the embryonal stages, it is evident that these Qur'ānic verses give an accurate description of the main stages the embryo encounters during creation and formation until delivery. It is noticeable that these changes coincide with the remarks of modern embryology, and truly express the external phenomena of change that results from internal change. The Qur'ānic descriptions contain expressions which people of different backgrounds can comprehend, whereas the current expressions employed in embryology used to describe these stages are in the form of numerical coding, so lacking any description. This proves the wonderful and miraculous nature of the Qur'ān, which could only have been revealed by the Omniscient. These facts were confirmed by the embryologist Professor Keith Moore and also other non-Muslim scientists.

Fourteen centuries ago, the Qur'ān was able to accurately describe the whole process of human creation. These descriptions now fit with the modern rules of science. Both now accord that the creation and development of the embryo are fulfilled in stages. As Allah says:

> *What is the matter with you, that you place not your hope for kindness and long-suffering in Allah — Seeing that it is He that has created you in diverse stages?* (71:13-14)

Non-Muslim scientists at the time of the Qur'ān's revelation believed that man was created from menstrual blood. Even as late as the seventeenth century, they still believed that the embryo was fully created from man's sperm, and that it then grew after entering the uterus. Thus they perceived man as a seed reduced wholly in that small drop of sperm. This idea remained as such until the eighteenth century when microscopes proved that sperm and ovum are both necessary for pregnancy. This was discovered so many centuries after it was first revealed by the Qur'ān. This shows that the Qur'ān is the word of a will that knows the creation of man down to its slightest detail. This will is Allah's, the Creator of man, Who says:

> *And say:'Praise be to Allah, Who will soon show you His signs, so that you shall know them.* (27:93)

He also says:

> *Soon will We show them Our signs in the (furthest) regions (of the earth), and in their own souls, until it becomes manifest to them that this is the Truth.* (41:53)

So says the Almighty Allah.

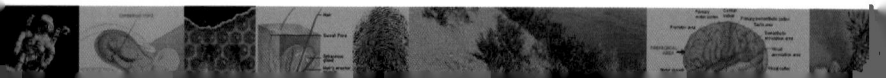

Chapter 2

The Sensation of Pain on the Skin

It was commonly believed, for several centuries, that the whole body is sensitive to pain. It was not clear then that there were specialized nerves in the body responsible for transporting pain and other sensations. Indeed, it is only recently that anatomy has discovered the role of these specialized nerve endings.

The most significant nerve sensations in the human body are:

- **Touch**: the corpuscles responsible for such sensation are called Meissners and Merkels corpuscles.
- **Pain**: this is transported by the nerve endings in the skin.
- **Heat:** this is the responsibility of Ruffini cylinder corpuscles.

Taking skin burns as a distinct cause of pain, burns can be divided into three types:

- **First degree (sun burns):** these affect the epidermis (see Figure 23) causing swelling and moderate pain. The phenomena of redness, swelling and pain usually disappear within two to three days, (see Figure 24).

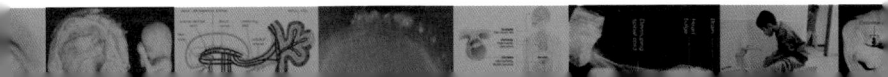

- **Second degree:** the epidermis and dermis are injured. Here, a detachment occurs between the epidermis and dermis, causing the collection of secretions between these two layers (see Figure 25). The injured person suffers severe pain, and an excessive increase of the pain sensation, due to irritation of the exposed nerve ending, particularly after the outburst of blisters. The skin starts to heal within 14 days as a result of the process of renovation and inversion under the skin.

- **Third degree:** the whole skin thickness is burned and perhaps the injury may reach the muscles or the bone. The skin loses elasticity and becomes rough and dry. In this case, the injured person does not feel much pain, as the nerve endings have almost been completely damaged due to burning (see Figure 26).

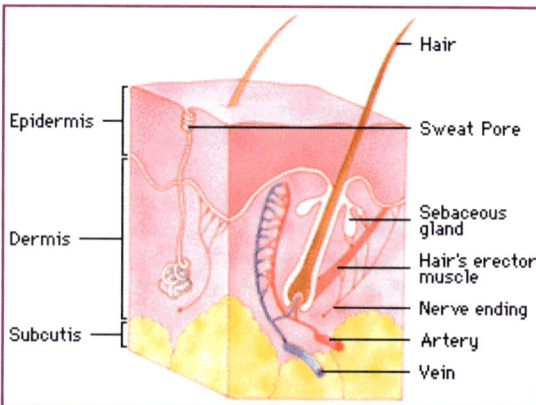

Figure 23: The nerve endings are exposed if the dermis and epidermis layers are injured

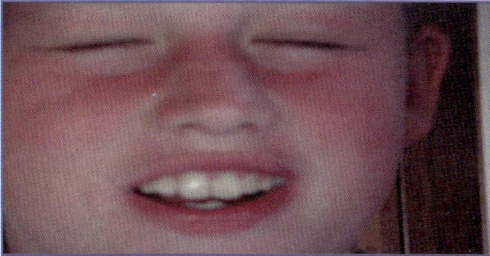

Figure 24: First degree burns (sun burn on the face)

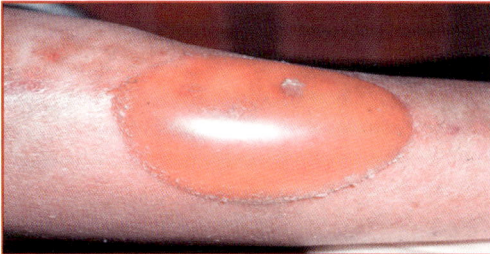

Figure 25: Second degree burns (a blister on the leg, which is very painful if burst)

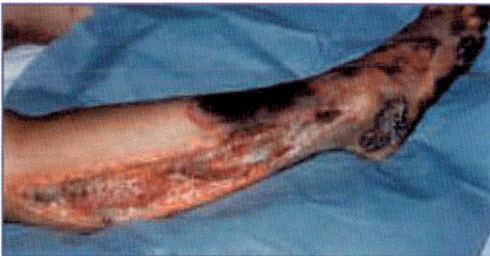

Figure 26: Third degree burns (a full thickness burn, which is not painful)

The Qur'ān states:

> *Those who reject Our signs, We shall cast into the Fire;*
> *as often as their skins are roasted through. We shall*
> *change them for fresh skins, that they may taste the*
> *penalty; for Allah is Exalted in power; Wise.* (4:56)

Allah did not say "as often as their skins are burned", as burning can be partial. Instead, He said: "as often as their skins are roasted through", i.e. totally burned with all this carries in the way of pain through the nerve endings. So, here, Allah associates the sensation of pain on the skin when it is roasted and burned totally, thus losing its structure and function. When the sensation of pain is lost, a new, fully composed and functional skin replaces the old one. The nerve ending responsible for the painful sensation of heat and burning performs and functions so as to make the unbeliever taste the punishment of being burned with fire over and over again.

Chapter 3

The Intestines

Anatomy has discovered that the small intestines are the longest part of the digestive system being about five metres long. The walls of the intestines consist of three layers:

1. **The external stratum** (serum stratum): its membrane is soft and wet due to the secretion of a serum liquid.
2. **The medium stratum** (muscular stratum).
3. **The internal stratum** (mucosa stratum): this consists of a mucosa plate and circular or ring folds full of villi, and contains intestinal glands and lymphatic vesicular.

It has been found that the abdominal cavity is lined with the peritoneum which is fed through the wall nerves feeding the skin, and the muscles of the chest and abdomen. These nerves are affected by touch and heat. The viscera are without pain or sensation producing nerves. Therefore, when the abdominal wall is anaesthetized locally, and the abdomen is open, no sensation of pain or disturbance is felt in the intestines if held, cut or even burned. But when the intestines are cut or perforated for any reason, its contents spill out into the cavity surrounding the viscera.

This is rich in sensitive nerves, hence the pain is then very severe and the patient's abdomen is in a state called 'Board Like Rigidity'. This is an emergency surgical state that requires an immediate operation. (See Figure 27)

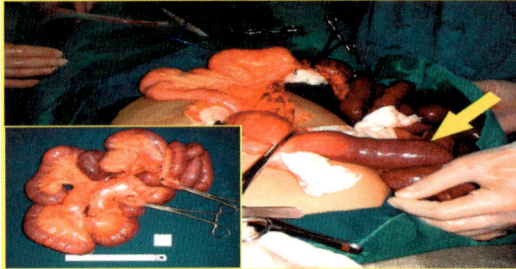

Figure 27: A perforated intestine causes severe abdominal pain

In the Qur'ān, Allah, the Almighty, says about the torment of Hell Fire:

[such are] given to drink, boiling water, so that it tears their bowels into (pieces). (47:15)

The Qur'ān threatens the unbelievers with hot water that tears their bowels. The reasoning underlying this threat has recently become evident. It has been discovered that intestines are not affected by heat. But if they are cut, hot water then spills out into the peritoneum which is fed through the wall nerves feeding the skin, and the muscles of the chest and abdomen. These nerves are affected by touch or heat, so the hot water, after the intestines are cut causes the highest degrees of pain.

So the outer torment felt in the skin, is different from that felt in the inner intestines, due to the difference in the nature of the skin structure. The feeling of former torment cannot be maintained unless the roasted skin is exchanged with a new layer, while in the case of the intestines, torment is felt only by cutting the intestines with hot water. This torment is, however, continuous:

For them [the unbelievers] will be the Fire of Hell; no term shall be determined for them, so they should die, nor shall its penalty be lightened for them. Thus do We reward every ungrateful one! (35:36)

In this way, the Qur'ān's scientific miracles are crystalized. The feeling of pain as perceived by medical facts is very much compatible with the statements made in the Qur'ān.

Chapter 4

The Importance of Hearing Over Sight in the Qur'ān

Allah the Almighty says:

> *And pursue not that which you have no knowledge of; for every act of hearing or of seeing or of (feeling in) the heart will be enquired into.* (17:36)

Furthermore:

> *You did not seek to hide yourselves, lest your hearing, your sight and your skins should bear witness against you; but you think that Allah knew not many of the things that you used to do.* (41:22)

Also:

> *Say: 'Think you, if Allah took away your hearing and your sight, and sealed up you hearts, who – a god other than Allah – could restore them to you?'* (6:46)

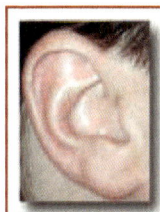

Figure 28:
Hearing comes before sight in the vast majority of verses in the Qur'ān!

So, what are the possible reasons behind advancing hearing over sight in Qur'ān? It is known that hearing develops before sight in the embryo stage, and furthermore that it is the first sense that functions in life. The function of hearing starts immediately the baby is delivered, contrary to the eyes which do not function at this initial birth stage. In other words, Allah the Almighty conveys to us that it is hearing that functions first. If a disturbing sound is produced near a newly born baby, it feels terrified and cries. But if a hand approaches the same baby, it does not move or sense any sort of danger. The ear is superior to the eye, as it does not stop functioning with sleep. Since the very beginning of life, the ear functions at the first instance after delivery, while some other organs may take days, or years to function. The eye needs light to see. Rays of light are reflected on things, then these enter the eye such that it can see things. If it is dark, the eye cannot function, but the ear can function day and night. The ear is also the link between man and the world. When Allah the Almighty decreed that the Men of the Cave sleep hundreds of years, He said:

Then We drew (a veil) over their ears, for a number of years, in the Cave. (18:11)

Hence, when their ears were not functioning, the Men of the Cave were able to sleep hundreds of years without any disturbance. Noisy daylight movements, contrary to night-time quietness, prevent man from sleeping deeply. Yet the ears never sleep nor lose their attention.

It is also to be noted that the word hearing comes before the word sight in the Qur'ān, except in one verse, which tackles Doomsday:

> *If only you could see when the guilty ones will bend low their heads before their Lord! (saying) 'Our Lord, We have seen and we have heard; now return us, (to the world) that we may do works of righteousness, for we do indeed (now) believe.'* (32:12)

In only this one verse does Allah forward the word see over that of hear. This because of the horrible scenes of the Day of Judgement which overwhelm people, and which they will see before they hear of, and Allah knows best.

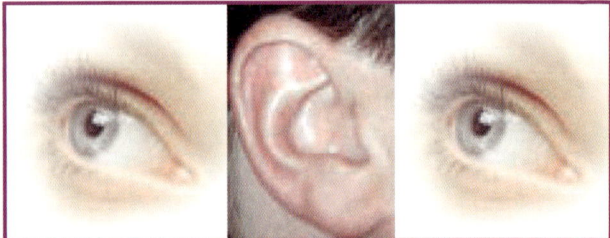

Figure 29: Why is it that in the Qur'ān the word ear is singular while eye is plural?

It is also noticeable that the word ear is always referred to in the singular form while the word eyes is in the plural. Allah says:

> *You did not seek to hide yourselves, lest your hearing, your eyes and your skins should bear witness against you; but you thought that Allah did not know many of the things that you were doing.* (41:22)

Furthermore:

> *Say; 'Think you, if Allah took away your hearing and your eyes and sealed up your hearts, who – a god other than Allah – could restore them to you?'* (6:46)

Why is it, in the Holy Qur'ān, that the word ear is always singular, while the word eye is plural? Why could it not be ears and eyes, or ear and eye?   Allah the Almighty, in such an accurate expression, seeks to reveal to us the precision of the Holy Qur'ān. Sight can be willingly controlled by man, as he can opt whether to see something or not. Man can close his eyes to the things he does not like to see, but he cannot do the same with his hearing, as he has no control over whether the ear hears or not.   In other words, when someone is in a room where ten people are talking, their voices will reach them whether they are willing or not. Sight also varies among people; someone sees something while another sees something else due to variations in their sight, while someone else closes their eyes and sees nothing. For hearing, we all share the same sound, if we are assembled in one place. Hence, eyes vary but ears stand singular.

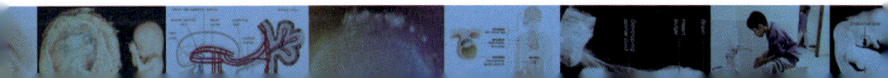

Chapter 5

What We See and
What We Do Not See

Are there really things around us that we cannot see? A quick look at the nature of light, being the tool of vision and sight, can help us understand this better.

- There is a difference between visible light and light in general.

- The light scale in general starts with less than 0.1 of a nanometre, as in the case of rays of short wave and high power (gamma rays), up to more than one kilometre, as in the case of long waves and low power (radio waves). (See Figure 30)

- Visible light is the light waves that man's eyes can receive and through which he can see things. This has no significant rate in the wave length scale of light or in electromagnetic waves, where normal light waves with their seven known colours reach a rate of 400-800 nanometres (A nanometre is one thousand-millionth of a metre) on the scale grade.

- Man with the help of visible light can see all around, as he can see microorganisms through microscopes and far celestial bodies through telescopes. Man was not able before the discovery of these two instruments to see more than his naked eye permitted. Man can presumably see all that which can be seen by visible light, regardless of whether it is minute or huge. This gives room to the question about other unseen worlds.

• What is the volume of these visible things in direct light waves in comparison with the things that cannot be seen or perceived by the human eye?

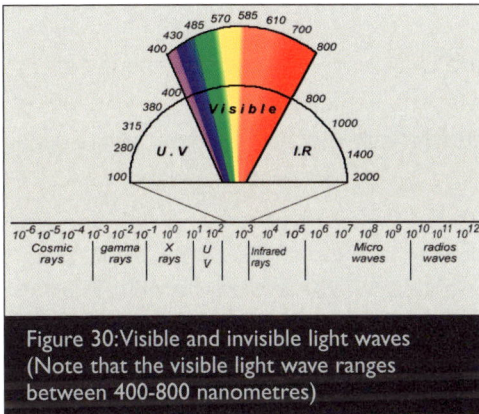

Figure 30: Visible and invisible light waves (Note that the visible light wave ranges between 400-800 nanometres)

Below are given the different types of famous rays and their existence on the wave length scale, arranged in an ascending order as per the length of wave and in a descending order as per the power range:

1. Gamma ray: its length is less than 0.1 of a nanometre, and is considered of the highest power.
2. X-ray: its wave length reaches up to 1 nanometre and is high in power and can penetrate many substances. It is commonly used in the medical field.

3. Ultraviolet ray: its wave length reaches up to 100 nanometres and originates from star explosions and the sun.

4. Visible light: the length of different waves range between 400–800 nanometres.

5. Infra-red ray: its length is 0.1 of the millimetre and is usually originated from hot substances and every living being. This ray is used by armies to locate targets – machineries and soldiers – that emit heat. Many snakes also use it to precisely determine their quarries.

6. Short waves or microwaves: these are used in telecommunications (especially in mobile phones), and commonly used in heaters. They are also used in guiding planes, and in determining the speed of traffic on roads.

7. Radio waves: these range between one metre to one kilometre in length and are originated from stars as other rays, as well as the lightning processes in clouds, and can be received by radio sets. They are used in wireless telecommunications in general.

The Qur'ānic miracle is thus crystalized, as Allah verily says:

> *So do I call to witness what you see, and what you see not."* (69:38-39)

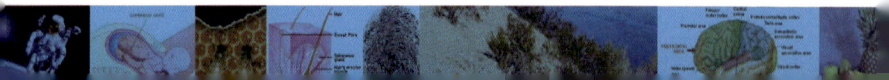

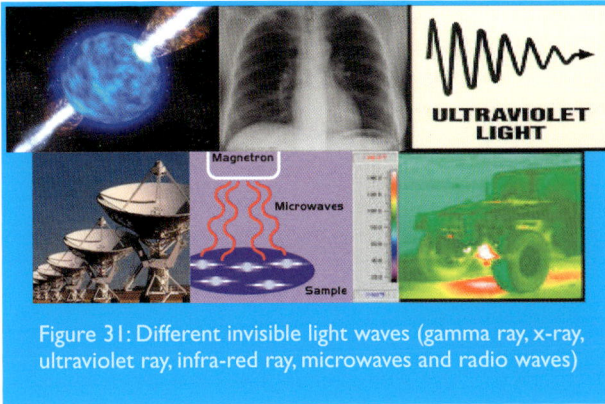

Figure 31: Different invisible light waves (gamma ray, x-ray, ultraviolet ray, infra-red ray, microwaves and radio waves)

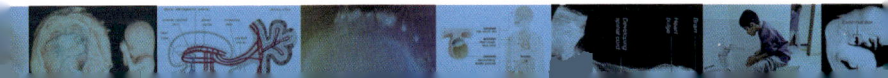

Chapter 6

The Origin of Creation: Clay and Water

In the Qur'ān, Allah reveals that the creation of man is a miracle. The first human being was created by Allah shaping clay into a human form and then breathing a soul into it. Allah says in the Qur'ān:

> *Your Lord said to the angels, "I am going to create a human being out of clay. When I have formed him and breathed My Spirit into him, fall down in prostration to him!"* (38:71-72)

Furthermore:

> *Ask their opinion: are they more difficult to create or the (other) beings We have created? We created them from sticky clay."* (37:11)

When the human body is examined today, many elements present on the earth are also discovered to be extant. Living tissues contain 95% carbon, hydrogen, oxygen, nitrogen, phosphorus and sulphur, with a total of 26 different elements. In another verse of the Qur'ān we are told:

We created man from an extract of clay. (23:12)

The Arabic word **sulāla**, translated as extract in the verse, means representative example, i.e. an essence. As we have seen, the information revealed in the Qur'ān 1,400 years ago confirms what modern science now tells us: namely, that the same elements as those found in the soilare are employed in human creation.

See the diagram next page which shows the distribution of the elements in a 70-kilogramme human being.

Water forms the main component of the human being, (over 70%) as indeed any other being. Allah says:

Allah has created every [living] creature from water. Some of them go on their bellies, some of them on two legs, and some on four. Allah creates whatever He wills. For Allah has power over all things. (24:45)

We made from water every living thing? Will they not then believe? (21:30)

It is He Who has created human beings from water and then gave them relations by blood and marriage. Your Lord is All-Powerful. (25:54)

Figure 32: The origin of creation: clay and water!

Element	Symbol	%	Weight
Macro-minerals			Gramme
Oxygen	O	65.0	43,000
Carbon	C	18.5	12,000
Hydrogen	H	9.5	6,300
Nitrogen	N	3.3	2,000
Calcium	Ca	1.5	1,100
Phosphorus	P	1.0	750
Potassium	K	0.35	225
Sulphur	S	0.25	150
Chlorine	Cl	0.15	100
Sodium	Na	0.15	90
Magnesium	Mg	0.05	35
Silicon	Si	0.05	30
Macro-minerals		%	Milligramme
Iron	Fe	0.01	4,200
Zinc	Zn	0.01	2,400
Copper	Cu	0.01	90
Boron	B	0.01	68
Cobalt	Co	0.01	20
Vanadium	V	0.01	20
Iodine	I	0.01	15
Selenium	Se	0.01	15
Manganese	Mn	0.01	13
Molybdenum	Mo	0.01	8
Chromium	Cr	0.01	6

When we look at the verses concerned with the creation of human beings and living things, we clearly see evidence of a miracle. One such miracle is the creation of living things from water. It was only possible for people to come across this information, clearly expressed in those verses, hundreds of years afterwards with the invention of the microscope.

All life forms need water in order to survive. Animals in dry regions, therefore, have been created with mechanisms to protect their metabolisms from water loss and to ensure maximum benefit from water use. If water loss takes place in the body for any reason, and if that loss is not replaced, death will result in a few days. The famous seventeenth century scientist Jan Baptista van Helmont discovered in the 1640s that water in the soil was the most important element for plant development.

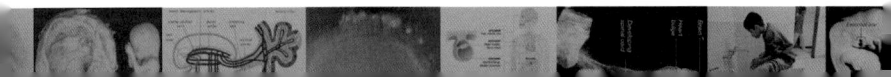

Chapter 7

Fingerprints

- Fingerprints are formed in the embryo at the fourth month, and remain fixed and distinct all along a human's life.
- Fingerprints are a record of curvatures that arise due to the fusion between the epidermis with the dermis.
- These curvatures differ from one person to another, and they never match or correspond among all humans.
- Fingerprints have become the best method to identify people. In 1858, the English scientist, William Herschel, pointed out that fingerprints differ as to their holders, thus rendering them a distinctive feature evidence for each person.

Allah says in the Holy Qur'ān:

I call to witness the Day of Resurrection. I call to witness the self-reproaching spirit. Does man think we cannot assemble his bones? Nay, We are able to shape again the tips of his fingers. (75:1-4)

Figure 33: Fingerprints are considered as distinctive feature evidence for each person.

- Physicians conducted wide anatomical studies on a large number of people of different nationalities and ages, and they were confronted with the scientific fact to which they bowed their heads in submission; namely, that it is impossible to render even two sets of fingerprints the same.

- The verse here speaks about the recreation of all fingertips, and not just one. The word fingertips refer to all hand fingers. So shaping them again after being scattered all over the universe on Resurrection Day is a sign of Allah's Almighty power. This is but one side of Allah's ability to resurrect people on Doomsday with their identifiable parts after annihilation.

- Therefore, it is not surprising that fingertips are one of Allah's signs that contain the secret of His creation. They certify to the entity of the person without any confusion, and are thus the most genuine testimony in this world and the Hereafter. The fingerprint is also a demonstration of Allah's greatness in shaping such lines on a very small space no more than a few square centimetres in size.

- Is this not a wonderful scientific miracle in which the power of Allah the Almighty is evident? Praise be to Allah the Almighty Who says:

  Soon will We show them Our signs in the (furthest) regions (of the earth), and in their own souls, until it becomes manifest to them that this is the Truth. (41:53)

Chapter 8

The Forelock

Allah the Almighty speaks of Abū Jahl (an inveterate enemy of Islam, who used to insult Prophet Muḥammad (peace be upon him) and his followers):

> *Let him beware! If he desist not, We will drag him by the forelock - a lying, sinful forelock!* (96:15-16)

The forelock is that lock of hair growing at or falling over the forehead. In explanation of Allah's verse: "We shall drag him by the forelock." Al-Farā' said: "it is by the forehead that He (Allah) shall seize Abū Jahl, to drag him, i.e. a sign of humiliation and disgrace."

Al-Alūsī said: "The forelock as described in the verse, indicates in the first place that this person is lying and sinful, and due to Abū Jahl's obstinate lying and sinning, every part of him is lying and sinning." Al-Alūsī also said: "The forelock is specifically mentioned here because the cursed Abū Jahl used to take good care of it by combing and perfuming it, and because seizing someone by the forelock is the utmost humiliation for any Arab."

- Some Qur'ānic commentators say: "The aim is not a
  lying forelock. Rather it is used metaphorically, not in
  the strict sense of the term, i.e. it is the forelock of a
  liar and a sinner. Since the forelock is the forehead, the
  description of lying refers to the possessor, as it could
  not be a place or source of lying.

- In his **Musnad**, Imām Aḥmad referred to the Prophet's
  hadith which points to the forelock. It was narrated
  that the Prophet said:

  > O, my Lord I am Your slave and the son of Your
  > slave and the son of Your bondmaid, my forelock
  > is in Your Hands…

  This ḥadīth reveals that man's fate is in Allah's Hands,
  as well as man's forelock, thus indicating, as the verse
  above does, that the forelock plays an important role
  in guiding and controlling man's behaviour.

- So, what is the reason underlying the use of the forelock?
  What is the hidden organ behind the forehead – that
  part which is responsible for the person's character
  and which controls man's behaviour and actions of
  truthfulness and lying, right and wrong, and which if
  subjugated can be controlled, as indicated in *Gray's
  Anatomy*, (eds. Warwick & Williams).

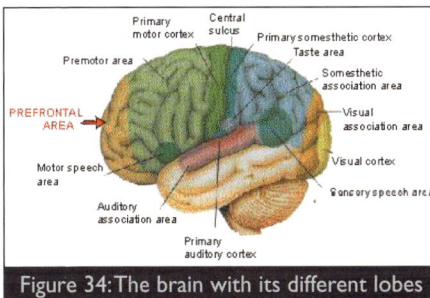

Figure 34: The brain with its different lobes

SCIENTIFIC FACTS

Man's brain contains the following main lobes:

- Frontal.
- Occipital.
- Temporal.
- Parietal.

- For each lobe, there is a functional role, which is at the same time complementary to the other body functions. Having dissected the forehead, the frontal lobe was found to be the part lying behind. The frontal lobe is characterized, as distinct from its animal counterpart, with the regions responsible for behaviour and speech being developed and distinct as per the anatomic and functional levels.

- The frontal lobe is a large lobe situated in front of the central groove, and contains five neurological centres that vary in location and position. (See Figure 34) These centres are as follows:

  i.   Primary motor area that helps move the voluntary muscles of the left side of the body.

  ii. Secondary motor area that helps move the voluntary muscles of the right side of the body.

  iii. Frontal eye field that helps move the eyes to the opposite sides compatibly.

  iv. Motor speech area of the broca that coordinates movements among the organs of speech, such as the larynx, tongue and face.

  v.   Pre-frontal cortex, which lies directly behind the forehead, and which represents the bigger part of the frontal lobe, and its function is responsible

for forming the person's character. It also has an effect in determining the ability of the person to take initiatives and form judgements.

- Since the pre-frontal cortex lies directly behind the forehead and deep under the forelock, it directs some of man's behaviour such as his propensity towards truthfulness and lying, right and wrong, and distinguishes among each of these characteristics.

- Electronic studies of brain and electric studies of organ functions have revealed that patients and animals subjected to damage of the frontal lobes often suffer a diminution of mental abilities. Any deficiency affecting the frontal lobe can change man's natural behaviour, so much so that man can suddenly and seemingly out of character perform evil deeds. As such, then damage to this area can be responsible for deterioration in moral principles, the memory, and the ability to solve mental issues.

- The frontal lobes of the brain are considered the centre for the initiative to lie. All mental activities of lying are conducted therein and are then transferred to messenger organs through the action of lying. Evil actions are also planned in this lobe before they are transferred to action organs. The lobe is also responsible for wrong actions being a centre of direction and control, as indicated in the *Encyclopedia Britannica*.

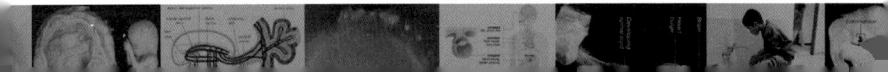

THE MIRACLE OF THE QUR'ĀN

The miracle in the above Qur'ānic verse and the hadith of the Prophet is that they refer very accurately to the frontal lobe, lying deep at man's forelock, as being the decision centre to control man's actions of truthfulness, lying, right, wrong, balance or perversion. This was only revealed by modern scientific studies in the second half of the twentieth century.

The brain is surrounded with three membranes, among which is the cerebral spinal fluid (CSF), which has the functions to protect, feed and cool. (See Figure 35)

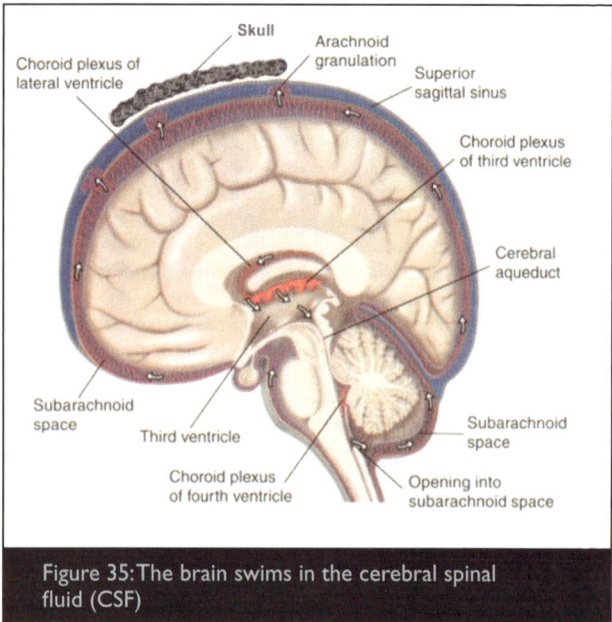

Figure 35: The brain swims in the cerebral spinal fluid (CSF)

It has been found that the brain inside the skull weighs 50 gm, although the real weight is 1,700 gm. The physical principle states that the volume of the object immersed in fluid is equal to the volume of displaced fluid. Therefore, it is of the Almighty Creator's decree that we do not feel the brain's weight, as it floats in the CSF, which originates from a special area in the brain called the corogy plexus, and rotates inside and comes out of another area such as the domestic water net. This cycle occurs five times a day.

So just as Muslims do before prayer, the brain receives ablution five times a day! We prostrate on the frontal lobe which is the centre of decision making. When prostrating and worshipping Allah, the Muslim's forelock is certified as truthful and right.

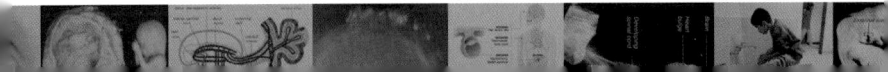

Chapter 9

How Man Copes in High Altitudes

Almost 100 years ago, medical researchers started addressing the functions of the human body when in high altitudes, and the effect of being in such a high atmosphere. Aero and space medicine provide much detail about this issue, in which the dyspnoea is explained in two main causes:

1. Less oxygen rates in high altitudes.
2. Decrease of air pressure.

The more we rise up from the surface of the earth, the more the air pressure decreases, thus leading to a decrease in the rate of air passage through alveoli pulmonis to the blood. A decrease of air pressure also leads to the distention of gases in the stomach and intestines that push the diaphragm upwards, thus pressing over and obstructing the extension of the lungs.

THE SYMPTOMS OF OXYGEN SHORTAGE

These are divided into four stages that relate to air pressure and the level of altitude and the rate of oxygen concentration in the blood:

Figure 36: The higher man climbs up in the sky the less oxygen is available

1. The stage of non alteration, i.e. from sea level to an altitude of three kilometers. In this stage, the symptoms of oxygen shortage are not present and sight is not affected at day time.

2. The stage of physiological adjustment, i.e. from an altitude of three–five kilometres. Body systems function in this stage in such a way that will not let the symptoms of oxygen shortage appear, unless the period of exposure to such a shortage is elongated, or the person exerts physical effort in such conditions. In such a case, rates of respiration, pulse, blood pressure and circulation increase in number and depth.

3. The stage of physiological disturbance, i.e. from an altitude of five–eight kilometres. In this stage, body systems, particularly the lungs, cannot afford to function properly or supply the quantity of oxygen sufficiently needed by tissue. Hence, symptoms of oxygen shortage appear. In this stage, a clear explanation is established for man's feeling of exhaustion, headaches, feeling the need to sleep, dyspnoea and chest tightness when traversing high altitudes. As a result of a decrease in air pressure, all air comes out of the lungs and the alveoli pulmonis, reducing the size of the lungs and chest (i.e. the chest becomes really tight).

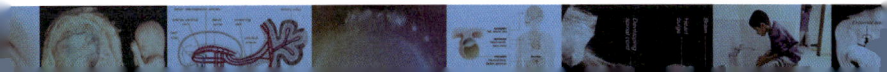

4. The stage of chest tightness, i.e. from an altitude of eight kilometres upwards. At this level, man loses consciousness totally due to the failure of the nervous system, and conditions become critical.

The Qur'ān which was revealed 14 centuries ago to Prophet Muḥammad (peace be upon him) states:

> *Those whom Allah desires to guide, He expands their chest to Islam; those whom He leaves straying, He makes their chest narrow, tight, as if they had to climb up to the skies.* (6:125)

Thus, this verse displays a miraculous similitude. Furthermore, it presents a scientific fact in a very eloquent and accurate style. The miraculous aspects of the verse are as follows:

1. When people first heard of the verse of man's climbing to sky (space), they considered it imagination, and that the Qur'ān regarded such ascension in a metaphorical manner. Actually, the verse fulfils a prophecy that came true centuries after it was first revealed.

2. The similitude is very accurate, as traversing high altitudes causes chest tightness and a feeling of suffocation. The more the ascension increases, the more tightness reaches the critical and difficult stage, so much so that respiration is no longer possible. Hence why oxygen cylinders are taken when ascending up into the sky, as in space craft!

Chapter 10

Medical References in the Light of *Sūrah al-Kahf*

The Qur'ānic Chapter 18, The Cave, or *al-Kahf* was revealed to answer a few questions which the **mushriks** (unbelievers) of Makkah had put to the Prophet Muḥammad (peace be upon him) in order to test him. One of their questions was: who were "the Sleepers of the Cave?" The disbelievers of Makkah were told that the story of the Sleepers of the Cave was clear proof of the creed of the Hereafter, as it shows that Allah has the power to resurrect anyone He wills even after a long sleep of death as He did with these youths (they slept over 300 years).

Allah the Almighty says:

> *Then We drew (a veil) over their ears, for a number of years, in the Cave (so that they heard not).* (18:11)

As we established earlier on, the sense of hearing is a physiological one: it does not stop functioning at the time of sleep (the sleeper can wake up at a nearby sound). This is because the 8th cranial nerve (which passes in the inner part of the ear) has two divisions: one for hearing and the other for equilibrium (position and movement of the head).

In the case of the Cave Sleepers, the physiological function of both hearing and equilibrium stopped, therefore, the Qur'ānic verse uses the expression "Drew (a veil) over their ears" rather than their hearing.

The other bodily functions were veiled, and the eye did not see though they were open:

> *You would have thought them awake, whilst they were asleep.* (18:18)

And their muscles did not move, although they were alive:

> *We turned them now on their right and on their left sides.* (18:18)

Their shape did not change although many years had lapsed. For example, upon waking, they were not aware of any facial changes:

> *They said: "We have stayed (perhaps) a day, or part of a day."* (18:19)

Their conditions, as such, are like that of preserving organs through cooling to cause metabolic inhibition, which is used extensively in the medical field to preserve donated organs (hearts, kidneys, cornea, etc) before transplantation into another body. Therefore, the sun inclines towards the right when rising up and towards the left when setting down, so that it will not strike them, while they are in a gap in the cave:

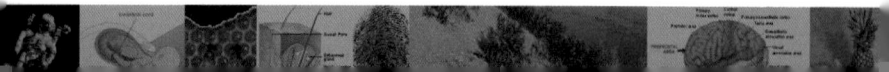

> *And you would have seen the sun, when it rose,*
> *inclining from their cave towards the right, and when it*
> *set, turning away from them on the left, while they lay*
> *in the open space in the midst of the cave. Such are*
> *among the Signs of Allah.* (18:17)

So, the coolness in this gap in the cave away from the heat of the sun that did not touch them, was sufficient to inhibit bodily metabolism for the preservation of their bodies during this long period. Had they only been asleep, they would have needed water and food to survive, and would have waken with the need to urinate after some hours. But Allah inhibited all their biological functions and preserved their bodies in a living shape. So, He said:

> *You would have thought them awake, whilst they were*
> *asleep.* (18:18)

Note, He did not say: "You would have thought them **dead**, as they lay sleeping", as the sign of awakening is the 'eye winking'. Allah preserved their eyes from blindness through blinking. For if the eye is kept closed for a long period of time it will go blind, because the optic nerve will shrink and die. Consequently, if it is kept open, the cornea will be affected with corneo-xerosis, and hence blindness. Therefore, this rare status of the sleepers would have aroused terror, if seen, as they were neither alive nor dead. They were asleep, yet their eyes were blinking:

> *Had you observed them surely you would have turned*
> *your back on them in flight, and been filled with terror*
> *of them.* (18:18)

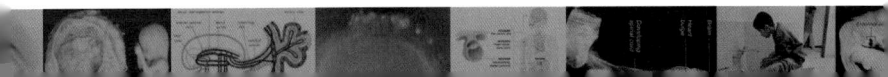

As Allah preserved their eyes through blinking, He also preserved their bodies from ulcers through constant turning:

> *While We turned them now on their right, and on their left sides.* (18:18)

This so that they would not be affected by pressure sores.

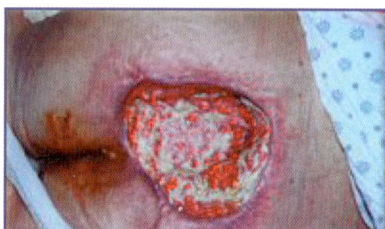

Figure 37: The pressure sore in the lower back due to lack of movement in a paralyzed patient

Chapter 11

An International Patent for an Eye-Drop Based on the Qur'ān

Inspired by the shirt of Yūsuf (Joseph), an Egyptian Muslim scientist, unprecedently, managed to manufacture an eye drop to treat cataracts. How? Inspiration came from Allah the Almighty's decription of Jacob's sudden blindness and, later, his equally sudden retrieval of sight.

> *And he turned away from them, and said: 'How great is my grief for Joseph.' And his eyes turned white with sorrow, and he fell into silent melancholy.* (12:84)

Whiteness, which is termed as cataract, affecting the eye is the opacity of the eye lens that prevents, partially or totally, the entry of light into the eye according to the degree of opacity.

CAUSES OF CATARACTS

1. A direct trauma to the eye lens.
2. High temperature.
3. Different types of radiation or flaring light, causing what is termed "radiation cataract".
4. Opacity due to a senile cataract, and diabetes mellitus that increases the concentration of fluids around the

lens and absorbs its fluid, causing the rapid presence of cataracts.

5. Severe grief causes the increase of the adrenalin hormone which in turn causes the increase of blood sugar, which is one of the causes of opacity in addition to the coincidence of grieving with weeping.

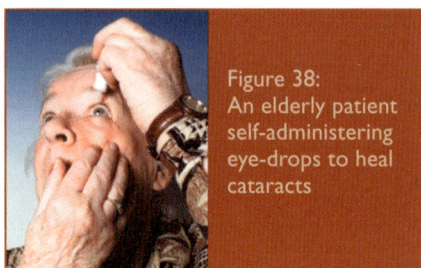

Figure 38:
An elderly patient self-administering eye-drops to heal cataracts

What the Prophet Joseph did, through a revelation from Allah, was to ask his brothers to take his healing shirt to their father:

"Go with this my shirt, and cast it over the face of my father: he will recover his sight; then bring your family here to me, altogether." (12:93)

When the caravan left (Egypt) their father (Jacob) said: 'I do indeed scent the presence of Joseph:' They said: 'By Allah! You are certainly wandering in your mind.' Then when the bearer of the good news came, he cast (the shirt) over his face, and forthwith he regained clear sight. He said: 'Did I not tell you I know from Allah that which you know not?' (12:94-96)

Hence is the beginning and the guidance!

What healing could be there in the Prophet Joseph's shirt? After meditation, the Egyptian Muslim scientist, Dr. Abdul Basit Sayed Mohammed, found himself preoccupied with man's ability to sweat. He then began to search the components of sweat. He immersed lenses extracted from traditional cataract surgeries in sweat. He found that a state of gradual transparency was established in these opaque lenses.

The second question he addressed was: are all sweat components effective in such a case or is this only one of its components? He later realized that one of its main components was the urea (goandin), and that this could be chemically prepared. The results of trial investigations on 250 volunteers revealed the removal of cataracts and the restoration of sight for more than 90% of patients. So, inspired by *Sūrah Yūsuf,* the Muslim scientist Dr. Abdul Basit Sayed Mohammed of the National Centre of Researches in Egypt was able to manufacture an eye-drop to treat cataracts. For this he obtained two international patents: The European International Patent in 1991, and the American Patent in 1993.

Allah the Almighty said:

We send down, of the Qur'ān, that which is a healing and a mercy to those who believe. (17:82)

Chapter 12

Breast-Feeding Your Baby

There are many benefits of breast-feeding, some of them are discussed here.

FOR THE MOTHER
- Protects against post-partum uteritis.
- Helps stop bleeding resulting from delivery, thus preventing loss of extra blood.
- Helps the uterine restore its normal size and place quickly after delivery.
- Prevents the recurrence of pregnancy with a rate of more than 98%, without contraceptives.
- Protects the lactating mother against breast and uterine cancer.

FOR THE BABY
- Breast-feeding protects the baby from viral infection, as it contains immunity agents.
- It protects against food allergy, as it is free of protein that causes such problems, and which is usually found in extracted and manufactured cows milk.

- It prevents shortage of calcium in the baby's blood, thus helping to construct strong bones.
- It provides spiritual and psychological benefits to the baby, as it helps build a well composed, righteous and straight personality, and strengthens the spiritual and passionate links between the baby and the mother.
- As revealed in research published in Pediatric Clinics of North America, February 2001, the mental abilities of babies who receive breast-feeding from their mothers are stronger and higher than otherwise, and the longer the period of breast-feeding, the higher the mental abilities are.
- It was shown that mother's milk also provides protection against cancer. After showing that the incidence of lymph cancer observed in childhood was nine times greater in formula-fed children, they realized that the same results applied to other forms of cancer. According to the results, mother's milk accurately locates the cancerous cells and later destroys them. Alpha-lac (alphalactalbumin), present in large quantities in mother's milk, is the substance that locates and kills such cancerous cells. Alpha-lac is produced by a protein that assists in the manufacture of the sugar lactose in milk.
- In addition to breast-feeding's practical benefits, the milk is always ready with steady and appropriate heat, fresh, sterilized and digestible. Furthermore, it saves money and time!
- Researchers indicated that breast-feeding alleviates the baby's fear of needle pricks and helps as an analgesic during painful operations such as circumcision.

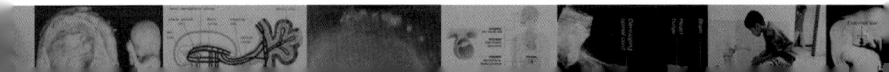

- A new theory has emerged in recent years indicating that the protein in cows milk can cause a biological reaction that destroys the pancreatic beta cells excreting insulin. This theory is supported by the high rate of the presence of cow milk proteins in the serum of children with diabetes in comparison with a study group of non-diabetic children.

Why is it that cows milk causes such harm in the months leading up to the second year, but thereafter disappears? In a study conducted in Finland, in 1994, and published in **Auto-immunity Journal**, the authors state that the protein of cow milk passes in natural form through the lining membrane of the digestive system which is not yet fully grown. As the enzymes of the digestive system cannot break the protein into amino acids, the protein of cow's milk enters as a complex protein and works as a catalyst to produce immunity agents in the body of the child. New references reveal that enzymes and the lining membrane of the digestive system and the kinetics of digestion and absorption do not attain to complete functioning except in the second year after delivery.

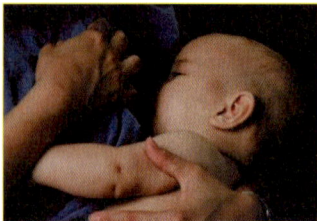

Figure 39: Many studies emphasize the benefits of breast-feeding in the first two years

In a very accurate scientific reference, the Qur'ān determines the period of lactation to be almost two years. In verse 14 of *Sūrah Luqmān*:

> *And We enjoined on man concerning his parents: his mother bore him in weakness upon weakness, and his weaning was in two years.* (31:14)

It is understood that lactation for two years is not a must, but a recommended period:

> *Mothers shall breast-feed their children for two whole years, for such as desire to complete the term.* (2:233)

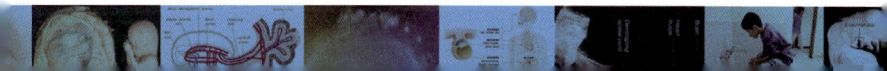

Chapter 13

The Miracle of Honey

Allah the Almighty says:

> *Your Lord taught the bees to build dwellings in the mountains and the trees, and also in the structures which men erect. Then eat from every kind of fruit and travel the paths of your Lord, which have been made easy for you to follow. From inside them comes a drink of varying colours, containing healing for mankind. There is certainly a Sign in this for those who reflect.* (16:68-69)

- Although honey is one of the most important products of the bee, it is not the only product. Honey wax, propolis, nectar, bee toxicant are cases in point that have been proved by experimental science to be of medical benefit.

- Honey contains more than 80 sugar vitamin materials and 15 sugar materials, particularly fructose, glucose, minerals, amino acids. There are also about 5% of unclassified materials.

- "Containing healing for mankind" is an explicit phrase indicating that honey is a treatment as well as a nutrient.

Figure 40:
A jar of honey
contains a
multitude of
benefits

THE BENEFITS OF HONEY

- It alleviates inflammation of the cornea if used locally on the eye.
- An antibiotic if used locally *in situ* of wounds and burns. Furthermore, it is used for the healing of wounds, specifically thanks to its ability to absorb moisture from the air. In this way, honey facilitates the healing process and prevents scarring, because it stimulates the growth of epithelial cells that form the new skin cover over a healed wound. Even in the case of large wounds, honey may eliminate the need for tissue transplantation.

Honey also stimulates the re-growth of tissue involved in the healing process. It stimulates the formation of new blood capillaries and the growth of fibroblasts that replace the connective tissue of the deeper layer of the skin and produce the collagen fibres that give strength to the repair.

Furthermore, honey has an anti-inflammatory action, which reduces the swelling around a wound. This improves circulation and thus hastens the healing process. It also reduces pain. Nor does honey stick to the underlying wound tissues, so there is no tearing away of newly formed tissue, and no pain, when dressings are changed.

Thanks to its aforementioned anti-microbial property, honey provides a protective barrier to prevent wounds from becoming infected. It also rapidly clears any existing infection from wounds. It is fully effective, even with antibiotic-resistant strains of bacteria. Unlike antiseptics and antibiotics, there is no impairment of the healing process through adverse effects on wound tissues.

Finally, some studies have shown that honey is a good treatment against the hospital infection bacteria 'superbugs', for example MRSA.

- As honey does not accommodate bacteria, this bactericide (bacteria-killing) property of honey is named 'the inhibition effect'. There are various reasons for honey's anti-microbial property. Some examples are: the high sugar content that limits the amount of water microorganisms need for growth, its high acidity (low pH) and composition which deprive bacteria of the nitrogen necessary for reproduction. The existence of hydrogen peroxide as well as antioxidants in the honey prevent bacteria growth.

- Everyone who wants to live a healthier life should consume antioxidants. Those are the components in cells that get rid of harmful by-products of normal metabolic functions. These elements inhibit destructive chemical reactions that cause spoilage of food and many chronic illnesses. Researchers believe food products rich in antioxidants may prevent heart problems and cancer. Strong antioxidants are present in honey: pinocembrin, pinobaxin, chrisin and galagin. Pinocembrin is an antioxidant that merely exists in the honey.

- A treatment for gastric and duodenal ulcers. As honey decreases the secretion of hydrochloric acid to a normal rate, it helps heal such ulcers, alleviates the related pains and reduces resultant cases of vomiting and colic. For the treatment to be effective, honey should be taken dissolved in warm water one or two hours before meals.

- A treatment for involuntary urination of beds. Such a disease can often have a psychic or neurotic cause. So, if the child is given one small spoon of honey before sleeping, this will have a positive effect, as honey is a sedative for the nervous system, thus helping the cyst to relax and expand during sleep. Concentrated sugar also helps to absorb water from the child's body.

- It supports blood formation: honey provides an important part of the energy needed by the body for blood formation. In addition, it helps in cleansing the blood. It has some positive effects in regulating and facilitating blood circulation. It also functions as a protection against capillary problems and arteriosclerosis.

- A treatment for colds, flu and pharyngitis.

- A treatment for cases of chronic hepatitis. As honey increases the liver stock of the glycogen material through the increase of blood glucose, it thus helps the liver to function properly and relieves it from unnecessary burdens.

- A treatment for insomnia and a sedative for nerves, as it contains some sedative and tonic substances, such as sodium and potassium at a reasonable rate.

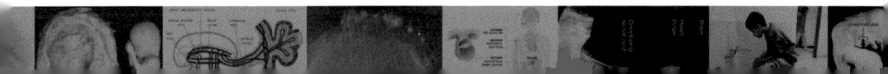

- A treatment for alcoholic poisoning. Honey is one of the main nutrients prescribed in hospitals and clinics for alcoholic addicts, as it protects the liver from alcohol poisoning. Fructose and the vitamin B group in honey helps oxidize the alcohol remaining in the body.
- A treatment for coughs.
- In cosmetics, a mixture of honey with lemon and glycerin is considered the best, old medical prescription for the treatment of skin cracking and roughness, inflammation and wounds around the lips, sun stroke, and dermal pigments. Many ointments and creams contain honey as a main element for the treatment of skin diseases.
- A treatment for muscular spasms resulting from sport or facial spasms and eyelids muscles, which disappear after having one large spoon of honey for three days after each meal.

It was narrated by al-Bukhārī and Muslim on the authority of Abū Saʿīd al-Khudrī that:

A man came to the Prophet Muḥammad (peace be upon him) and said: "My brother has some abdominal trouble." The Prophet said to him: "Let him drink honey." The man returned to the Prophet and said: "O Messenger of Allah! I let him drink honey, but it caused him more pain." The Prophet said to him; "Go and let him drink honey." The man went and let his brother drink honey, then returned and said: "O Messenger of Allah, it did not cause him anything except more pains." The Prophet then said: "Allah has said the truth, but your brother's abdomen has told a lie. Let him drink honey." So

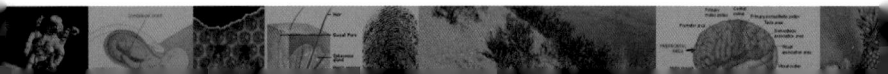

he made him drink honey and he was cured. It can easily be seen from this information that honey has great healing properties. This is undoubtedly one of the miracles of the Qur'ān, which Allah, Who is Exalted in Power, has revealed.

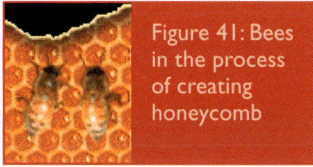

Figure 41: Bees in the process of creating honeycomb

Another interesting point regarding the female honey bee is also made in the Qur'ān:

Your Lord taught the bees to build dwellings in the mountains and the trees, and also in the structures which men erect. Then eat from every kind of fruit and travel the paths of your Lord, which have been made easy for you to follow. From inside them comes a drink of varying colours, containing healing for mankind. There is certainly a Sign in this for those who reflect. (16:68-69)

In honey bee colonies where each of the many bees is assigned a specific task, the only exception is the male honey bee. The males neither contribute to the defense of the hive nor its cleaning, nor to the gathering of food, or making the honeycomb and honey. The only function of the male bees in the hive is to inseminate the queen bee. Apart from reproductive organs, the males possess almost none of the features possessed by other bees and it is, therefore, impossible for them to do anything but fertilize the queen. The worker bees carry the entire load of the colony. Although they are females like the queen, their ovaries possess no maturity. This renders them sterile. They have several duties: cleaning the hive, maintaining the larvae and the young, feeding the queen and the males, producing honey, constructing the honeycomb and repairing it, ventilating the hive and safeguarding it, gathering supplies like nectar, pollen, water and resin, and storing these in the hive.

In Arabic, there are two different usages for verbs. By means of their usage, it is possible to determine whether the subject is female or male. As a matter of fact, the translated verbs into English (the underlined words) used for the honey bee are used in the feminine verb (in Arabic) format in the Qur'ānic verses. Based on this, the Qur'ān indicates that the honey bees that make the honey are females.

We should not forget that it is impossible for this fact to have been known during the time of the Prophet Muḥammad (peace be upon him). Yet, Allah illustrated this fact about bees and in the process revealed to us yet another miracle of His Qur'ān.

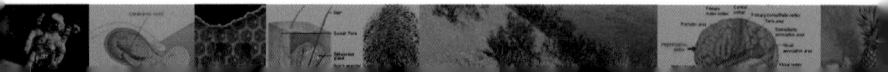

Chapter 14

Carrion, Blood and Pork

Allah says in the Qur'ān:

> *He has only forbidden you dead meat, and blood, and the flesh of swine.* (2:173)

He the Almighty also said:

> *Forbidden to you are carrion, blood and flesh of swine, and that which has been hallowed to other than Allah, and that which has been killed by strangling, or by a violent blow, or by a headlong fall, or by being gored to death; and that which has been partly eaten by a wild animal-excepting that you have sacrificed duly...* (5:3)

THE PROHIBITION OF EATING CARRION

What is the reason behind totally forbidding dead meat? It has been proved on a conclusive scientific basis that the body of a dead animal reserves blood with all its sediments and toxins, particularly those present in the arterial bloodstream. Blood can then prevail in the tissues and thus the toxins start to function in all body cells, thus

the dead body changes colour, becoming darker, and the superficial veins are filled with blood, and blood circulation stops with no chance of leaking outside the body. Thus, the dead body becomes a spoilt deposit for diseases and microbes. The work of decay then starts in the body, affecting the meat in colour, taste and smell. So the meat of dead bodies is foul and far from good. Allah says:

> *They will question you what is permitted them. Say; 'The good things are permitted you....'* (5:4)

Due to these decaying enzymes, the dead meat loses all its nutrients and becomes valueless. Allah says:

> *This Qur'ān is not such as can be produced by other than Allah; on the contrary, it is a confirmation of (revelations) that went before it, and a fuller explanation of the Book – wherein there is no doubt- from the Lord of all the Worlds.* (10:37)

Figure 42:
A dead cow

KINDS OF CARRION
- Strangled: it has been scientifically proved that in an animal that has been strangled oxygen is not allowed to pass into its lungs, and so toxic carbon dioxide, as well as poisonous secretions accumulate in its body.

- Killed by a violent blow, i.e. cattle beaten to death by a stick or stones.
- Killed by a headlong fall, i.e. falling from a height.
- Killed by being gored to death, i.e. by another animal.
- The remnants of cattle partly eaten by a wild animal. This is prohibited for a great divine reason. Modern medical science has recently discovered that germs and microbes are transferred to the prey when grabbed by the wild animal's claws, thus causing diseases to transfer to whoever eats the prey's meat. Wild animals in general are infected with a disease that lies in their mouths and saliva, which in turn are transferred to the body of the prey, causing great harm to eaters of such meat.

THE PROHIBITION OF BLOOD

Blood in a living creature possesses two main functions. First, it transfers nutrients absorbed by the intestines such as proteins, sugars, and fats, as well as vitamins, hormones and oxygen and all other vital necessary substances to body organs and muscles. Secondly, it carries harmful substances in the animal body for disposal through urine, sweat or stools. If the animal is diseased, microbes are multiplied in its blood, using it as the media for moving from one part to another, and this is where hazards lie. If man drinks blood, all these microbes and excretions are carried to man, thus leading to many diseases such as hyper-uremia leading to renal failure, or hyper-ammoniaemia leading to hepatic coma. Furthermore, many germs carried by blood cause irritation to the membranes of the stomach and intestines. Hence they induce disease.

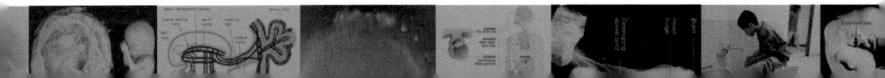

For these reasons, Islam's legal method of slaughter dictates that the animal be cleared of blood after slaughtering, so that cattle's blood is not allowed by any means to enter the human body. This was revealed long before microscopes were invented by man, or information about such microbes and germs had reached man's knowledge.

THE PROHIBITION OF SWINE (PORK)

The Muslim is submissive to Allah's commands even if His underlying wisdom has not yet revealed itself.

> *The answer of the believers when they are summoned to Allah and His Messenger, that he may judge between them, is that they say; 'We hear and we obey;' those – they are the prosperous.* (24:51)

Figure 43: Eating pork is prohibited in Islam

Some recent Western studies have revealed that eaters of the flesh of swine (pork) carry the same characteristics as swine.

The Qur'ān adopts the preventive method, whether for medical or social diseases, and their causes. This is much better than the claims of the West and their inventions in the field of treatment which require huge sums of money, with no guarantee as to positive results. No matter how the West is trying to beautify the image of the swine, by providing the most up to date equipment for caring and cleanliness, this will not counteract the fixed reality discovered by their own scientists of the worms and diseases contained in the body of swine as compared with other animals. Eating pork is harmful to health in a great many respects. This harm still persists today, despite all the precautions that are taken. First and foremost, no matter how clean the farm and environment on which it is raised may be, the pig is not by nature a clean-living animal. It often plays in, and even eats, its own excrement. Due to this and its biological structure, the pig produces much higher levels of antibodies than other animals. In addition, far higher levels of growth hormone are produced in the pig compared to those in other animals and human beings. Naturally, these high levels of antibodies and growth hormones pass across to and collect in the pig's muscle tissue. Pork meat also contains high levels of cholesterol and lipids (the rate of cholesterol is almost 15 times higher than its rate in cows). It has been scientifically proven that these significant amounts of antibodies, hormones, cholesterol and lipids in pork represent a serious threat to human health.

The existence of above-average numbers of obese individuals in the populations of countries such as the USA and Germany, in which large quantities of pork are consumed, is now well-known. When exposed to excessive quantities of growth hormone as a result of a pork-based diet, the human body first puts on excessive weight and then suffers physical deformations.

Another harmful substance in pork is the trichina worm. This is frequently found in pork and when it enters the human body, it settles directly in the muscles of the

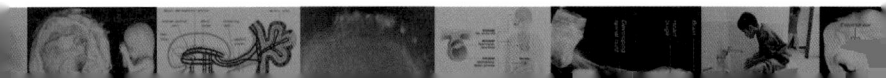

heart and represents a possibly fatal threat. Even though it is now technically possible to identify pigs that are infected with trichina, no such methods were known in earlier centuries. That meant that everyone who ate pork risked infection by trichina and possible death.

Another disease is the tapeworm which is transmitted from the pig to man's intestines. It is a few metres long, and has about 22-32 hooks in the head, with which it clings to the intestinal wall. The larva leaks into the bloodstream and settles in one of the body organs such as the heart, the liver or the eye, where it vesiculates. Settling in the brain, its favourite place, the worm can cause epilepsy. The worm from a cow conversely has no such grievous power to roam and travel with its larva in the human body.

All these reasons are just a part of the wisdom in our Lord's prohibition on the consumption of pork. Moreover, this commandment provides complete protection from the harmful effects of pork under any conditions.

Until the twentieth century, it was impossible to be aware of the danger posed to human health by pork. The fact that the Qur'ān, revealed 14 centuries ago, warns against this harm which has been incontrovertibly revealed with modern medical equipment and biological testing, is one of the miracles demonstrating that the Qur'ān is the revelation of Allah, the Omniscient. Despite all the precautionary measures and inspections that take place in modern-day pig rearing, the fact that pork is physiologically incompatible with the human body and is a variety of meat harmful to human health has not altered.

> *Surely this Qur'ān guides to the way that is straightest...*
> (17:9)

Chapter 15

The Importance of Fruit: Before or After?

- Doctors advise that, prior to eating, man should start with soft and easily digestible food in order to prepare the oral glands secreting the peptic juice (saliva amylase) or the glands in the stomach and duodenal to start functioning gradually in digesting food. Minutes later, man can start eating the main dish.
- A slice of fruit or dates are cases in point of soft food.
- The Qur'ānic statement mentions fruit in advance of meat, in a remarkable reference to the previous meaning when addressing the state of believers in paradise:

And such fruits as they shall choose, and such flesh of fowl (chicken) as they desire." (56:20-21)

Figure 44: Fruit before meat aids digestion

Chapter 16

The Health Benefits of Ablution (*Wuḍū'*)

Allah says:

> *O believers, when you prepare for prayer, wash your faces, and your hands (and arms) up to the elbows, and wipe your heads (with water), and wash your feet up to the ankles. If you are defiled, purify your whole bodies* (5:6)

Figure 45: Ablution for physical and mental well-being

ABLUTION IS THE WEAPON OF THE FAITHFUL

- Ablution is not just a case of cleaning the external organs several times a day before prayers. The psychological and spiritual impact felt by the Muslim after ablution is deeper than words can express, particularly when perfecting ablution. Ablution plays an important role in the life of the Muslim, as it keeps him always in a state of vitality, vigilance and fitness. The Prophet said:

"He who performs ablution, and perfects it, his sins will come out of his body, till they pass out from under his nails."

- The process of washing the organs usually exposed to dust is no doubt of great significance to public health. These body parts are exposed all day long to numerous microbes counted in millions in every cubic centimetre of air. These microbes are in a constant offensive state against the human body at the exposed areas of skin. In ablution, microbes are taken by a surprise sweep from the surface of the skin, specially with perfect massaging and enough pouring of water, as guided by the Prophet. Following such a process, no dirt or germs are left on the body except what Allah decrees.

- Rinsing the mouth. Modern science has proved that rinsing the mouth protects the mouth and throat from inflammation and the gums from suppuration (pyorrhoea). It also protects and cleans teeth by removing food remnants.

- Sniffing the nose. Washing and sniffing the nose keeps the nostrils clean and free of inflammation and germs, thus reflecting positively on the health status of the whole body.

- Washing the face and hands. Washing the face and hands up to the elbows is of a great benefit in removing dust and microbes as well as sweat from the surface of the skin. This also cleans the skin from the fatty substance secreted by skin glands, and which is usually a very suitable place for the proliferation and sustenance of germs.

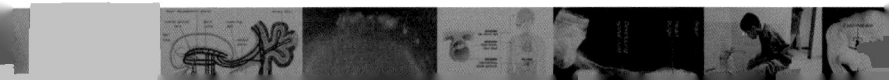

- Washing the feet. Washing one's feet with a massaging motion leads to a feeling of quietness and complacency that engulfs the Muslim after ablution.
- Other secrets. Scientific research has proven that blood circulation in the upper limbs, from the hands to the forearms, and in the lower limbs, from the feet to the legs, is weaker than it is in other organs, being peripheral to the centre of regulating blood circulation, namely, the heart. So washing these limbs with a massaging effect at every ablution helps strengthen the blood circulation in these parts, thus increasing the body's vitality. Science has proven the effect of the sun's rays, particularly ultra violet ones, in causing skin carcinoma. This effect decreases very well with the consequence of ablution, as it constantly dampens the surface of the skin with water, particularly the parts exposed to such rays. This helps protect the surface and internal layer cells of the skin from the rays' harmful impact.

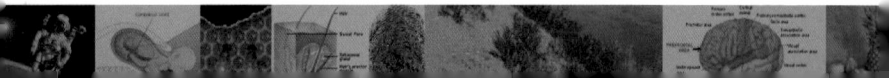

Chapter 17

Prayer: A Healing Tonic for Body and Soul

Allah says:

> *Seek Allah's help with patience and prayer: it is indeed hard, except for those who are humble.* (2:45)

THE HEALTH BENEFITS OF PRAYER

- Prayer helps release the burden of the soul and expands the chest. In prayers, which are the best deeds, the heart becomes connected to Allah the Almighty. The Prophet said, as narrated by Ibn Mājah and Al-Ḥākim on the authority of Thawbān:

  Be it known to you that your best deeds are prayers.'

- Prayers are surely a healing for the soul. It is confirmed that the Prophet, if afflicted with grief, would hurry to prayer:

> *Prayer forbids indecency and dishonour. Remembrance of Allah the greatest (thing in life) without doubt. And Allah knows the things you work.* (29:45)

- Prayers help adjust the rhythm of the body. Modern scientific research has proven that Muslims' prayer timings correspond with that of the physiological activities of the body. Thus, prayers are considered as the orchestrator that adjusts the rhythm of the whole body. In his book **Seeking cure from prayers**, Dr. Zaheer Rabeh indicates that cortisone is the active hormone that increases acutely in the human body with the approach of dawn, and is associated with the rise in blood pressure. In this way, man is much more active after dawn prayer, between 6-9 am. Thus, the time after prayer is considered the best time for hard work and seeking one's livelihood. The Prophet Muḥammad (peace be upon him) was quoted as saying:

"O Lord, give benediction to my *umma* (nation) at the early morning time."

Ozone, which has an invigorating effect on the nervous system, and muscular and mental activity, reaches its highest levels in the air at such a time.

Contrary to this is the forenoon time *(Ḍuḥā)*, in which secretion of cortisone reaches the minimum limits; leading man to feel exhausted with the stress of work, and the need to have a rest. This is almost seven hours after getting up. Here comes the time of noon *(Ẓuhr)* prayer, which provides quietness to the exhausted heart and body, and following which man seeks to get an hour of sleep to rest and reinvigorate himself, in what is termed as a *qaylūla* (nap) before (*'Aṣr*), afternoon prayer. Such a short sleep was mentioned in the Prophet's saying: "Get help with **suhoor** (the meal before dawn) for fasting, and with

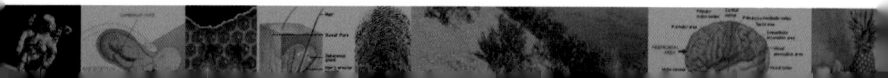

qaylūla for **Qiyām** (night) prayer." He also said: "Have *qaylūla,* as satans do not have it." It has been proven that the human body at this period generally encounters a hard time, where an increase occurs in an anesthetic chemical substance secreted by the body that has the effect of tranquilizing, and so inciting man to sleep. The body, seven hours after waking, is at its lowest levels of concentration and activity. So if man ignores sleeping at this time, much of his neuromuscular compatibility decreases all day long.

Then comes the 'Aṣr, afternoon prayer to reinvigorate the body once again. Adrenalin is then raised in the blood; causing activity in the body functions, particularly the cardiac one. 'Aṣr prayer thus has a great effect in preparing the heart and the body to accept this sudden state of activity, which can cause serious trouble to cardiac patients due to the sudden transfer of the heart from an inert to an active state. Allah says:

> *Guard strictly your (habit) of prayers, especially the middle prayer, and stand before Allah in a devout (frame of mind).* (2:238)

Most Qur'ānic commentators agreed that the middle prayer is 'Aṣr prayer. With the discovery of the increase of the adrenalin hormone at this time, the reason behind this Qur'ānic command of keeping up 'Aṣr prayer becomes crystal clear. Performing 'Aṣr prayer at a designated time, alongside other extra prayers, reinvigorates the heart gradually so that it functions more effectively after an inert state. The rest of one's bodily organs and senses are in deep

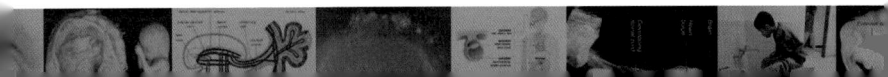

concentration in prayer, making it easy for the heart and the hormones to adjust to the normal rhythm of the body which climax at that time.

Then comes the **Maghrīb**, sunset, prayer. Contrary to what happens early in the morning, cortisone decreases and the activity of the body starts to diminish. With the transfer from daylight to night darkness, melatonin increases encouraging relaxation and sleep, and causing laziness to engulf the body. Here, prayer comes as a transitional station.

The '**Ishā**', early night prayer is the last station in the course of the day, wherein the body is transferred from a state of activity and mobility to a state of seeking sleep with the spread of darkness and the increase of melatonin secretion. Therefore, it is commendable to delay '**Ishā**' prayer to the time just prior to sleep so that all man's preoccupations are finalized, and sleep ensues. The regular secretion of melatonin is closely related to sexual and mental maturity, which is the consequence of following a fixed programme and a way of life. Therefore, we find that adherence to performing prayers on time is the best way to guarantee an integral compatibility with daily activities. It also leads to the highly efficient functioning of human bodily systems.

- Prayer prevents varicosing. Varicose veins on the legs are a common dysfunction, which takes the shape of large, zigzag veins filled with blood of a changed colour all along the lower limbs. Dr. Tawfiq Elwan, a Professor in Alexandria's Faculty of Medicine, Egypt, indicated that

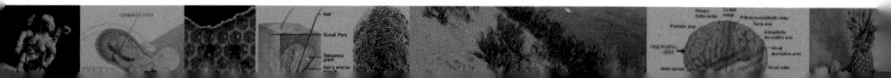

with the meticulous observation of prayer movements, it was found that prayer is distinguished by a wonderful measure of smoothness, harmony and coordination, represented in standing, kneeling (*rukū'*), prostration (*sujūd*) and sitting between every two prostrations. A scientific study on the measure of pressure exerted on the walls of the saphenous vein at the ankle joint found that a great decrease in that pressure occurs during kneeling; such pressure being reduced by almost one-half. As for the state of *sujūd*, the average pressure becomes very slight. Naturally, this decrease provides full rest to that vein, which is greatly exhausted by long periods of standing. *Sujūd* also helps the blood circulate in the same direction as earth's gravity, as blood from the soles of the feet to the cardiac muscle now pour smoothly and easily from top to bottom. This process greatly reduces the vein pressure over the feet dorsum. Amazingly, the reduction in pressure from standing to prostration represents around 80%. Consequently, the risks of having varicose veins, which rarely affects those performing prayers regularly and properly, are diminished.

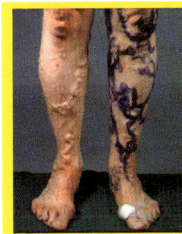

Figure 46:
Varicose veins
in both legs

- Prayer for strengthening bones. Bones pass through two consecutive stages: anabolism followed by catabolism and so on in a continuous manner. In our youth and growth, man's anabolism increases, so bones become longer and stronger. After maturity and with the advance of age, catabolism takes over, with the amount of bone decreasing and becoming more fragile, and the spine bows due to the vertebra's collapse, shortness and weakness. The activity and the strength of bones are the outcome of the amount of pressure and pulling exercised by the muscles and tendons, which stick to the bones, during flexion and extension.

    It has recently been proven that an electric current with two different poles runs inside the bones; affecting the distribution of cell functions such as anabolism and catabolism. The current also determines, at large, the aspects of these cells' activities. The experiments proved that in laziness and rest, the electric current is diminished, leading the bones to lose their componential materials, thus they become thin and weak. Experiments also revealed that during travel to space where gravity is totally absent, muscles become weak and bones thin because of the inability to resist the burden of the earth's gravity. Hence, it was deduced that complete rest causes the bones to shrink, as the absence of movement activates catabolism cells, and weakens anabolism cells, with a resultant reduction in bony material.

- The performance of 17 units (**rak'ah**) of obligatory prayer, plus some extra prayers, strengthens man's bones, and forces him to perform bodily movements for

no less than one hour daily. This happens throughout a Muslim's life, for Muslims never abandon their prayers.

- Prayer is a regular and simple exercise performed at different times of the day. It helps the body maintain its viability, especially the cardiac system and blood circulation.

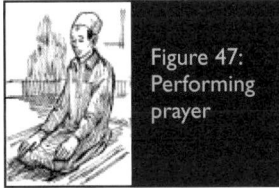

Figure 47: Performing prayer

- Prayer is a psychological therapy that helps calm the soul and relieves all tension. The most significant reason for this is that man feels that all his problems are very small in the face of the Greatness and Capability of the Creator who handles this large universe. The Muslim, after finishing his prayer, has thrown all his problems and worries aside, as he has deputized the Merciful Lord to manage and relieve him of these. Prayer also helps remove all sources of tension because of the constant changes of movement involved. It is known that such changes lead to important physiological relaxation, therefore, the Prophet (peace be upon him) commanded that the Muslim when afflicted by a state of anger should resort to prayers. It has been proven that prayer has an immediate effect on the nervous system, it calms agitation and maintains balance. Prayer also constitutes a successful treatment for insomnia resulting from dysfunction of the nervous system.

Chapter 18

The Medical Benefits of Fasting during Ramaḍān

Fasting during Ramaḍān is an obedience to Allah the Almighty, who said in His Honourable Book:

O believers, fasting is prescribed for you, even as it was prescribed for those who were before you, that you may learn self-restraint. (2:183)

Fasting is a prescribed duty, and a private relation between man and his Lord. It is also something for which Allah guarantees His reward. It was narrated in a **ḥadīth qudsī** that Allah says:

Every act of the son of Adam is for him, except fasting. It is meant (exclusively) for Me and I give reward for it.

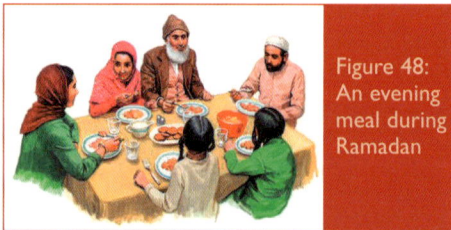

Figure 48: An evening meal during Ramadan

In 1994, the first conference on the health benefits of fasting during Ramadan was held in Casablanca, Morocco. Around 50 research papers from all over the world were discussed by Muslim and non-Muslim researchers.

SOME OF THE HEALTH BENEFITS OF FASTING DURING RAMAḌĀN

- **Resting the digestive system**. Ramaḍān represents a period of rest for the digestive system, which is responsible for the metabolic process of food. Consequently, the liver also takes a rest as it is the main factory of food metabolism. To achieve this benefit, Muslims should adhere to the tradition (Sunna) of the Prophet by abstaining from taking too much food after breakfast. The Prophet (peace be upon him) said:

  "The son of Adam never fills a bowl worse than his belly. Some bites are enough for man to prop his physique. Had he wished otherwise, then one third for his food, and one third for his drink, and one third for his breath."

  It is of benefit to the body that the break of fasting begin with some dates (as indicated in Prophetic tradition). Dates are rich in glucose and fructose, which contain a great caloric benefit especially for the brain, and are useful in raising the level of sugar in the blood gradually, thus reducing the feeling of hunger and the need for large quantities of food.

- **Moderate weight loss**. During fasting, the consumption of sugars decreases, as does the level of sugar in the blood stream. This makes the body burn excess sugars that have been stored there in order to provide the

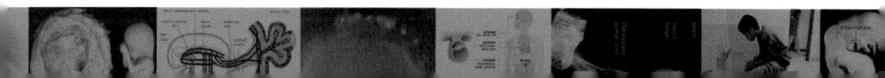

necessary calories for metabolism. Glycogen stored in the liver, and fats in tissues are decomposed and transferred into calories and energy needed by the body. This results in a moderate loss of body weight. Therefore, fasting is considered of great value for overweight people and stable non-insulin diabetics.

- **Decreases cholesterol levels in the blood**. Several studies have proved that cholesterol levels in the blood during fasting, as well as the rate of precipitation on the walls of arteries are decreased. This in turn reduces the chances of cardiac and cerebrovascular accidents, and prevents the raise of hypertension. The shortage of fats in the blood also helps reduce gall stones choledocus. The Prophet said: "Fast! You will be healthy."

- **Rest to the renal system**. Some studies have revealed that abstaining from drinking water for about 10-12 hours per day is not necessarily bad; it is rather useful in many cases. The concentration of liquids in the body means there is a sufficient liquid reserve, and as long as the person has no renal lithiasis complaint, both kidneys are rested from the process of waste disposal. The Prophetic tradition mandates that **suḥūr** (the meal before dawn) be delayed and **fuṭūr** (breakfast) be expedited, thus reducing the time period of dehydration as much as possible; moderate dehydration in any case is something most bodies can tolerate. This shortage of liquids leads, in turn, to a moderate decrease in blood pressure and again this is something that most people can tolerate. It is also of use to those complaining of hypertension.

- **Educational and psychological benefits**. Fasting during Ramadan is useful as it has a restraining power over the soul's whimsies, urging it to abandon bad habits, especially when the smoker is obliged to abstain from smoking even if only temporarily. This also applies to drinking too much coffee and tea. The psychological benefits are numerous. The fasting person feels complacent, attains mental and psychological rest, refrains from all that disturbs the integrity of his fasting, and maintains the proper behavioural controls that reflect positively on the general community. The Prophet said:
  "Fasting is restraining. When anyone of you is fasting, he should refrain from obscene language or any acts of ignorance. And if anyone slanders him or quarrels with him, he should say; 'I am fasting, I am fasting.'"
- Several studies have also revealed that the crime rate in Islamic countries decreases during Ramaḍān .

Figure 49: A typical Ramadan greeting

Chapter 19

The Qur'ān: A Healing and a Mercy!

Allah the Almighty said:

> We send down (stage by stage) in the Qur'ān, that which is a healing and a mercy. (17:82)

- **The Qur'ān restores the soul to calmness.** The results of researches conducted over a group of volunteers from the USA who were subject to a recitation of the Holy Qur'ān were striking. A trace of a tranquilizing effect was recorded for 97% of participants. Although many of these volunteers did not know Arabic, they nonetheless experienced involuntary physiological changes that led to noteable alleviation in the acuity of tension they were observed to possess in their nervous systems prior to the experiment. Furthermore, an EEG experiement during Qur'ān recitation revealed that while listening to the Qur'ān, the encephalic waves moved from the fast pattern of vigilance, 12-13 waves per second, to the slow pattern, 8-18 waves per second; indicating a state of deep calmness. Non-Arabic speaking people felt reassured, quiet, and relaxed when listening to Qur'ānic verses, in spite of their inability to

understand their meaning. This is one of the miracles of the Holy Qur'ān. The Prophet revealed this miracle by saying:

"People assembled in one of the houses of Allah (mosques), and who recite and study the Book of Allah (among themselves), find that a tranquility prevails over them, and that a mercy encompasses them, and that the angels surround them, and that Allah mentions them in the presence of those near Him."

- **A healing from diseases.** It is commonly known that the Qur'ān removes tension and covers the soul with tranquility and contentment. Yet is this effect of the Qur'ān limited to our souls only? Afterall, Allah said:

We send down in the Qur'ān, that which is a healing and a mercy to those who believe. (17: 82)

Figure 50:
The Qur'ān
is a healing
and a mercy

So how can the Qur'ān be a healing for our bodies? It is medically asserted that tension and worry lead to a deficiency in the body's immune system. The more the psychological and nervous condition of man is not stable, the more likely he is to suffer disease invasion. Hence, the explanation becomes crystal clear: the Qur'ān is a healing for our bodies just as it is a healing for our souls and spirits. The Qur'ān regains the balance of the believer's nervous and psychological systems: the more one recites and listens

to it, and contemplates its meaning, the more one's bodily immunity and internal defenses are safeguarded. In this way, believers find sanctity from disease. With the Qur'ān's luminous powers, all microbes and germs attacking the body in consecutive waves are resisted.

Dr. Ahmed El-Kadi conducted research in the USA on three groups of Americans who did not speak or understand Arabic. He connected them to instruments for measuring biomedical functions such as blood pressure, heart pulse, EEG, myography, and sweat tests. He recited some Qur'ānic verses for the first group, and ordinary sentences of everyday Arabic for the second group, while the third group was a control group resting in a state of relaxation. He found that the physiological changes for the first group listening to the Qur'ān's recitation enjoyed significant improvements over the other two groups (These results were announced by the Islamic Organization for Medical Science.)

Verily said the Almighty Allah:

> *Had We sent down this Qur'ān on a mountain, you would have seen it humble itself, and split asunder out of fear of Allah. Such are the similitudes which We propound to men; that they may reflect.* (59:21)

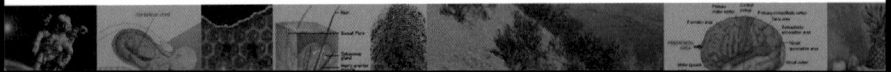

Conclusion

The Qur'ān cannot be produced by any creature. It is the word of the Almighty God, the Originator of everything and the One Who encompasses everything with His knowledge. How could any creature reveal such scientific facts and signs, as contained in some of the Qur'ān's verses, providing information that was impossible for anyone to know at the time of its revelation? The Qur'ān, with its accurate description of all scientific facts that accord with the modern rules of science, affirms that this was revealed by Allah. Man has begun to unfold these signs with the help of modern technology centuries after they were revealed by Allah. The Qur'ān is the word of Allah Who has created everything and Who knows the slightest details of His creation. Who could have inspired the Prophet Muḥammad (peace be upon him) with such scientific truths in such a noble and well contrived language except Allah?

Although they possessed and knew the tools of the Arabic language, the unbelievers of Makkah were challenged to produce just one verse like those found in

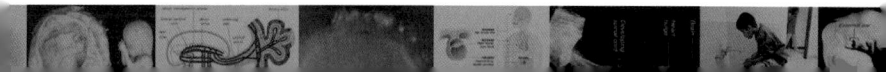

the Qur'ān. Yet, up till now and till Doomsday the challenge still stands:

> If the whole of mankind and jinns were to gather together to produce the like of this Qur'ān, they would never produce its like, even if they backed up each other with help and support. (17:88)

Allah also says in the Holy Qur'ān:

> If it had been from other than Allah, they would surely have found many inconsistencies in it. (4:82)

With the passage of ages, every word of the Qur'ān still reveals the divine and miraculous nature of this Holy Book. For the believers, this is a message to hold fast to their divine book and receive it as their only guide in this world and the Hereafter:

> And this is a Book which We have revealed as a blessing: so follow it and be righteous so that hopefully you will receive mercy. (6:155)

For the unbelievers, it is a call to open their minds and hearts to the word of Allah, the Holy Qur'ān, and contemplate and ponder this last revelation to mankind. Yet, Allah remarks:

> Say, 'The Truth is from your Lord; so let him who will believe, and let him who will disbelieve.' (18:29)

And:

No Indeed! It is a message of instruction: so let those who will keep it in remembrance. (80:11-12)

And say: 'Praise be to Allah, Who will soon show you His signs, so that you shall know them.' (27:93)

Soon will We show them Our signs in the (furthest) regions (of the earth), and in themselves (souls and bodies) until it becomes manifest to them that this is the Truth. (41:53)

References

The Holy Qur'ān.

Bucaille M., *The Bible, The Qur'ān and Science.*

Guyton and Hall, *Textbook of Medical Physiology,* 10th edition.

Moor K., 'A Scientist's Interpretation of References to Embryology in the Qur'ān', *Journal of the Islamic Medical Association,* 1986: vol.18, pp 15-16.

Moor K. and Persaud T., *The Developing Human.* (6th edition), 1998.

Newing A., *Light, visible and invisible, and its medical applications,* Gloucestershire Medical Physics Service, UK, 1999.

Singhal A., Cole T.J. *et al,* 'Breast milk feeding and lipoprotein profile in adolescents born preterm: follow-up of a prospective randomized study', *Lancet,* 2004 May 15; 363(9421):1571-8.

Snell R. *Clinical Anatomy* (3rd edition), 1986.

Papers presented in The Seventh International Conference on Scientific Signs in the Qur'ān and Sunnah, Dubai 22-24 March 2004.

Islamic Medicine On-Line web site (Dr. Sharif Kaf Al-Ghazal) http://www.islamicmedicine.org

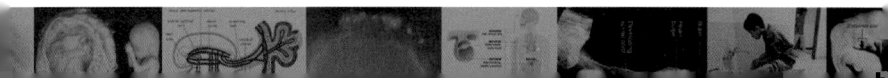